CORPORATE TIDES

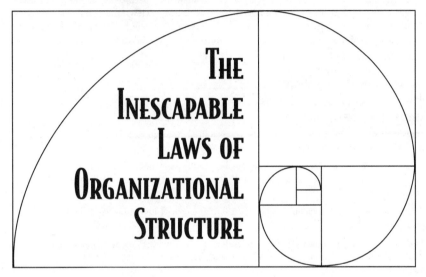

THE
INESCAPABLE
LAWS OF
ORGANIZATIONAL
STRUCTURE

ROBERT FRITZ

Berrett-Koehler Publishers
San Francisco

Berrett-Koehler Publishers, Inc.
155 Montgomery Street
San Francisco, CA 94104-4109
Tel: 415-288-0260   Fax: 415-362-2512

ORDERING INFORMATION

Individual sales. Berrett-Koehler publications are available through most bookstores. They can also be ordered direct from Berrett-Koehler at the address above.

Quantity sales. Special discounts are available on quantity purchases by corporations, associations, and others. For details, contact the "Special Sales Department" at the Berrett-Koehler address above.

Orders for college textbook/course adoption use. Please contact Berrett-Koehler Publishers at the address above.

Orders by U.S. trade bookstores and wholesalers. Please contact Publishers Group West, 4065 Hollis Street, Box 8843, Emeryville, CA 94662; 510-658-3453; 1-800-788-3123; Fax 510-658-1834.

Printed in the United States of America

 Printed on acid-free and recycled paper that is composed of 85% recovered fiber, including 15% postconsumer waste.

Library of Congress Cataloging-in-Publication Data
Fritz, Robert, 1943–
     Corporate tides : the inescapable laws of organizational structure
/ Robert Fritz
      p.   cm.
    Includes bibliographical references and index.
    ISBN 1–881052–88–5 (alk. paper)
    1. Industrial organization.   2. Corporate reorganizations.
3. Organizational effectiveness.   I. Title.
HD38.F726   1996   96–15508
658.1'6—dc20   CIP

98 97 96   10 9 8 7 6 5 4 3 2

To my friend and colleague
Peter Senge

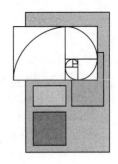

Table of Contents

PART 3 STRUCTURAL THINKING 143

PART 4   DESIGNS FOR GREATNESS   175

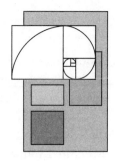

Preface

*. . . so I drew these tides of men into my hands
and wrote my will across the sky in stars.*

T.E. Lawrence

Billions of dollars have been wasted on attempts to change organizations through programs that were doomed before they started. These attempts were launched by dedicated people who often adopted change systems that had proven themselves in other organizations. Often these programs had support throughout the organization, from senior management to the rank and file. The companies' best and brightest devoted themselves to mastering techniques of TQM, or reengineering, or principles of organizational learning. But to little avail.

With so much focus on change, why is there so little successful change? One penetrating answer: Change has been imposed on top of existing inadequate organizational structures. Building on a weak foundation is always a risky business.

If we were to build a skyscraper on a weak and inadequate foundation, eventually the building would fall because the underlying architecture would not have supported it. Of course, no one would do that. People who put up buildings know about structural principles. Also, there are building codes used to regulate the structural integrity of buildings, so they will stand, even when abused by hurricanes or earthquakes. Alas, the same type of common understanding about the structural integrity of buildings does not yet exist in the world of organizations. If we design our organizational structures poorly, no one from City Hall is going to complain.

In order for us to succeed at change, we must understand the underlying structure of the organization. We must create strong, well-structured foundations. The key to success is designing change that is structurally sound. The key to disaster is ignoring the organization's structure.

Like the tides, the natural forces in play in the world do not change because we might like them to, or because we are sincere or dedicated, or because we are able to be above their influence. As Sir James George Frazer wrote about those who lived by the sea who are moved by the water's ceaseless ebb and flow, "(They) trace a subtle relation, a secret harmony, between its tides and the life of a man." We are tied to the rhythms of life in ways that are often invisible. But we can come to know the tides, and by the use of such knowledge, to navigate them successfully.

Organizations have their own tides that must be navigated when traveling to their desired destinations. We must understand the forces in play if we are to reach our goals and fulfill our purpose. When we don't understand these forces, we may find that we willfully forge our way to disaster. We cannot ignore the dominance of the natural world for long before we inadvertently violate its laws.

While natural laws and principles influence our organizations, we are not victims of them any more than is the sailor a victim of the natural elements. These laws and principles can be observed and learned. We can then work *with* them rather than against them. And that is what this book is about: working with the structural forces in play so that we may build organizations that are able to reach their destinations successfully.

As we will see from this book, all organizations have success, but not all success succeeds in the end. The power of structure is that it will determine the outcome in ways that are consistent with its laws. Not only do we want success to succeed long term, but we want it to be the foundation on which to build further strength and vitality into the organization. Without an understanding of structure, this would be very difficult.

The great organizational leaders have understood structure, although often on the level of instinct, intuition, or talent. But the *feel* they had for structure could not be translated to the rest of the organization. When these leaders left their organizations, the structural integrity they had created was dismantled slowly but surely, and then the organization was no longer able to live up to its past glory.

When such a change happens, people point to the prevailing conditions as the cause of trouble. They do not understand the inescapable structural laws that are in play. Symptoms, rather than causes, are addressed. This begins an oscillating cycle of recurring problems, and temporary shifts from progress to difficulties. Without understanding the inescapable laws of organizational structure, people attempt to change their organizations through the latest management approach: reengineering, TQM, organizational learning, self-organization, and so on. These interventions can rip an organization apart when members fail to understand what they are confronting— an inadequate organizational structure. Like a body rejecting an implanted organ, the organization will reject the change.

The organization pays a terrible price for the defeat, not only in money, but also in lost hope, alignment, and vitality.

The purpose of this book is to make clear the power and beauty of structure, so that people can design their organizations well—so that their best efforts can ultimately succeed.

If your car began to skid on the ice, your instinct would be to jam on the brakes. The *instinct* is correct—to regain control and stop the car. But the action would not help. If anything, it would make matters worse. People often have the right instincts about their organizations, but they are not able to translate their instinct into workable action. This book is designed to help the reader translate the right instincts into right actions—actions that work well structurally.

The purpose of this book is to make visible what is often invisible, so that we can build the type of organizations we want. It is divided into four major sections: Principles of Structure; Elements of Design—From Organizational Oscillation to Advancement; Structural Thinking; and Designs for Greatness. The first section of the book sets out certain themes, and later sections develop them.

In the first section, we explore the major structural principles that impact organizations. Chapter 1 introduces the notion of *the inescapable laws of organizational structure.* (In fact, nine laws appear as the book unfolds.) These laws help us to understand why organizations behave the ways they do. By knowing these laws, we can design our organizations in ways that take structure into account. Chapter 1 also introduces two distinct types of organizational patterns—*oscillation* and *advancement.* Much of this book is designed to help organizations move from structural oscillation, in which repeating cycles plague the company, to structural advancement, in which the organization moves toward success.

Chapter 2 describes general principles about structure and introduces structural *axioms.* The difference between axioms and our nine laws is this: The axioms are about structure in general, while the laws apply specifically to organizations. For us to better understand organizational structural laws, the axioms provide important background. This chapter also introduces structural tension, the major structural mechanism used to create organizational success.

Chapter 3 introduces structural conflict, the structure that causes organizations to oscillate. Chapter 4 shows how problem-solving approaches to structural situations fail to change the underlying causal forces in play, and produce or reinforce oscillation.

Chapter 5 explores the most common organizational structural conflicts, and Chapter 6 reveals the key to addressing these structural conflicts.

The Elements of Design section mixes structural insights with how-to's. Chapter 7 discusses the principle of thematic unity and contrasts self-organizing systems with ones that are organized thematically. Chapter 8 explores the business strategy in its relationship to the structure of the organization. Chapter 9 tells us how to change from an oscillating structure to one that advances, and how to design the entire organization so that it reinforces its aims. Chapter 10 reports on those who have used the structural approach in their organizations.

The next section introduces structural thinking. One element of creating workable organizational structures is our ability to be fluent in the reality that confronts us. This section focuses on ways we can enhance our ability to be clearer and more accurate about reality. Chapter 11 discusses frame of reference, and how we need to change it to see the patterns and shapes that reality forms. Chapter 12 introduces the process of structural thinking. It also addresses questions of how to observe reality objectively.

The final section of the book, Designs for Greatness, is both a *how-to* and a discussion of critical elements of organizational success. Chapter 13 explores the subject of vision in its relationship to structure; Chapter 14 addresses the critical element of organizational leadership; and Chapter 15 discusses motivation, reward systems, and human involvement. Chapter 16 takes a structural look at the learning organization, and Chapter 17 addresses organizational greatness itself.

This book is dedicated to my friend and colleague Peter Senge. With his quick and penetrating mind, his natural goodness, his wonderful charm and wit, and his profound quest to reach beyond the haze of illusion, he is truly one of the great people on the planet. He is the seminal figure of the field of organizational learning, and his books have influenced an entire generation of managers and management thinkers. But beyond his great accomplishments—and he is one of the most accomplished people I know—there is Peter, the human being. To be in his presence is an enriching experience whether we talk about philosophy or baseball, or just "hang out."

The reader who is fluent in Peter's work will recognize both great commonality and some differences between our two approaches. We share a keen interest in system and structure, and the hope that organizations can rise to greater heights of human accomplishment, not only in the products and services they offer, but also in the ways they relate to their people and to the world. Whenever Peter and I have co-led seminars we have played with ideas like jazz musicians "trading phrases." Peter is generative, creative, and when he talks or writes I take his work seriously.

Readers of *The Fifth Discipline,* or *The Fifth Discipline Fieldbook,* will easily recognize the points where I come to very different conclusions from Peter. In fact, the subjects of structure and system, while similar and compatible, are not identical. Sometimes structural dynamics has led me to quite different conclusions than system dynamics has led Peter. It is hoped that these differences can add to the public dialogue, rather than entrench people into dogmatic positions. I am grateful that Peter has made his case so well, even when his point of view is in variance with mine, because it helps to define the area of meaningful exploration. So thank you, Peter, for all of your momentous work.

Finally, this book describes a new type of consulting—*structural consulting*. For the past fifteen years, we have developed a specialized type of consulting that focuses on structural causality. Structural consultants are trained to identify what forces are in play in any situation, and then work with these forces to help restructure the organization—or even a person's life. Structural consulting is a technical skill, similar to mathematics or music, and those who are identified as structural consultants in this book have had extensive training to earn the title. I would like especially to thank my wife, colleague, and partner in life Rosalind Fritz. While I invented structural consulting, she was the next person to master it. Rosalind then developed the first comprehensive approach toward teaching it and trained other consultants. Without Rosalind's work, structural consulting would not have been available for others to learn.

This book is written for the manager on every level of the organization, and especially for those who are involved with leadership or change management. The hope is that you will be able to use the principles of this book to sail the corporate tides with wisdom and mastery. Godspeed.

Acknowledgments

There are many people who have contributed their talents, insights, wisdom, and energy to this book. And I am grateful to all of them. I am grateful to you, Jacques de Spoelberch, friend and literary agent, for your untiring work as champion of *Corporate Tides,* in particular, and my literary endeavors, in general. Over the years, and through many book projects, you have always been a tremendous support, colleague, and mentor.

I am grateful to the many structural consultants with whom I work. You are forging a new frontier that helps us all discover a new land. I am grateful to the many companies who have been the first to employ the structural approach in their organizations over the years. You have proven the power and good business sense of structural thinking.

I am grateful to you, Steven Piersanti, publisher of Berrett-Koehler, for your support of the project. Not only did you lend editorial support. I am grateful to Charles Dorris, who served as the major editor for this book. Your insight was superb, you skill masterful, and your impact great. Thank you, Charles! And thank you, Elizabeth Swenson, production director, for overseeing the process of turning the manuscript into a book. And I am grateful to you, Detta support. I am grateful to Charles Dorris, who served as the major editor for this book. Your insight was superb, your skill masterful, and your impact great. Thank you, Charles! And thank you, Elizabeth Swenson, production director, for overseeing the process of turning the manuscript into a book. And I am grateful to you, Detta Penna, for your special gift of book design, and for the way you applied your gift on behalf of this book. And thank you, Peter Penna, for your elegant illustrations. And thank you, Judith Johnstone, copyeditor, for the way you helped turn my most clumsy sentences into lovely phrases that expressed just what I was trying to say. And thank you, Katherine Lee, for proofreading the book cover to cover. And speaking of covers, thank you, Cassandra Chu, for your brilliant cover design.

And many thanks to Berrett-Koehler's marketing team, a group of crackerjack professionals, who know how to bring a book to market in ways that are truly consistent with the book itself. This is rare in your industry, and as an author, I am grateful. The team includes Patricia Anderson, director of marketing; Robin Donovan, promotion manager; Kendra Armer, marketing coordinator; Valerie Barth, publicity manager; and Kristen Scheel, sales manager.

Thank you, Robert Carlson and Karen Mathieu of The Fritz Consulting Group staff, for you dedication and untiring work on behalf of this book. You guys are great, and I am glad you're on our team.

I am also grateful to Alan Mossman, who had written the index for all of the British editions of my books, and now, for this current American edition. Not only is Alan a fine consultant, he also writes a "mean" index that, I must admit, I thoroughly enjoyed reading.

I also am grateful to the entire Berrett-Koehler staff, who not only have been personable and professional, but who were consistently hospitable to Rosalind and me during our visit to the Berrett-Koehler offices.

And speaking of my wife Rosalind: To you I am grateful beyond anything I could ever say in words, even though I love trying to say it to you. You are my best friend, colleague, inspiration, and love, and I don't think it's a secret to any who know us how much I adore you.

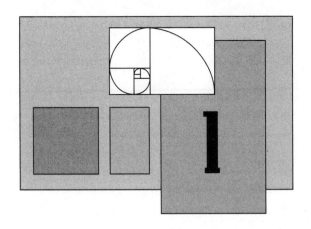

Principles
of
Structure

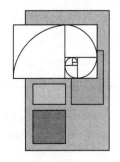

CHAPTER 1

The Inescapable Laws of Structure

Organizations follow inescapable structural laws. They do so because they must. They have no choice about it. This is as true for the successful organization as it is for the dysfunctional organization. So when an organization downsizes, then within two years hires back many people it had eliminated, or when it attempts to expand a market for its product, then finds higher sales have led to lower profits, or when it ignores plans made and "committed" to, or when it seems to resist needed change efforts—in all of these cases, the organization is simply following structural laws that produce inevitable patterns of behavior.

On the other hand, when organizations succeed at growing their markets, product bases, and organizational capabilities, they are following the *same* structural laws as organizations that fail. Both successful and dysfunctional organizations may have highly intelligent and capable people, well-thought-out strategies, excellent products, and dedicated and caring team players. So why are some organizations more successful than others? And, if they are following the same inescapable structural laws, where does choice come into play?

Our choices are not found in which structural laws we follow or which laws we violate. Choices are found in the way we structure our organizations. However, we usually do not structure our organizations consciously; we do it inadvertently. Smaller systems grow into larger systems, management is fragmented by division of labor. Departments and divisions become entrenched as power systems. Rewards reinforce contradictory values, conflicts of interest grow, and policies become bureaucratic. No one wanted it that way. No one, with malice aforethought, designed an organization to be inflexible, reactionary, and self-defeating. However, no matter how good intentions may be, organizations must be true to structural laws that govern them, and any change efforts that do not take these laws into account are likely to fail. Happily, the converse of that statement is true: Organizations that take structural laws into account when redesigning themselves are likely to succeed.

What structure *is* will be extensively discussed in Chapter 2, as well as throughout the rest of the book, but a brief definition here may be helpful: *Structure is an entity* (such as an organization) *made up of individual elements or parts* (such as people, resources, aspirations, market trends, levels of competence, reward systems, departmental mandates, and so on) *that impact each other by the relationships they form. A structural relationship is one in which the various parts act upon each other, and consequently generate particular types of behavior*. Structural laws govern the behavior of the organization. Understanding the inescapable laws of organizational structure will enable us to accomplish two important desires:

- To understand why the organization is the way it is.

- To redesign the organization so it can be what we want it to be.

Organizational Advancement and Oscillation

An organization produces from tens of thousands to millions of actions in pursuit of its goals. Coordinated or not, these actions produce overall effects that fall into one of two very different categories—structural *advancement* or structural *oscillation*.

THE FIRST LAW OF ORGANIZATIONAL STRUCTURE

Organizations either oscillate or advance.

This distinction is truly as black-and-white as it sounds. An organization is predominately one that advances or one that oscillates. Any type of action (TQM, organizational learning, reengineering, for example) occurring in an organization structured to advance has an entirely different effect than it would in an organization structured to oscillate. In both types of organizations there are instances of success. But the consequences of success are quite different. In structural advancement, success ultimately breeds long-term success; in structural oscillation, it doesn't.

Structural Advancement

When an organization advances, its accomplishments serve as a foundation for further aspirations.

Advancement describes moving from somewhere to somewhere else. When we throw a ball, it moves from our hand to where it lands. From one condition, to another.

In our organizations we want our actions to move us from an actual state (the current situation), to a desired state (our goals and aspirations)—movement that resolves once we achieve our ends.

The word *resolution implies movement coming to an end.* In the most effective organizations, there is example after example of resolving behavior. Action is first generated, then comes to an end once a desired outcome is achieved. Project teams complete assignments, write reports, prepare budgets, carry out advertising campaigns, and produce products. Countless repetitions of resolving behavior are linked together when management coordinates individual acts into an organizational tapestry of effective strategy.

Simultaneous and overlapping incidents of resolving behavior reinforce each other beautifully, leading to an organizational state of alignment. When this is true, enormous feats are accomplished. Well-structured organizations produce networks of resolving behavior that amplify the magnitude and scope of the enterprise. They have synergy. They advance themselves.

In such an organization, each person's actions count, contributing to the energy and talent of the entire enterprise.

To almost anyone who has worked in a corporation, this situation sounds Utopian. Most organizations are not structured to bring out the best performance in their members or the company itself. Why? Because the other type of behavior structure produces is *oscillation*.

Structural Oscillation

Oscillating behavior is that which moves from one place to another, but then moves back toward its original position. In an organization that oscillates, a period of advancement is followed by a reversal. Success and progress precede nullification and decline. The reversal is an inevitable product of the progress that came before it. In an oscillating organizational structure, success will lead to retrogression, not by anyone's choice but because it must.

To demonstrate the difference between advancement and oscillation, I often use two of my daughter's toys: a small Barbie car, and a doll's rocking chair. First, I push the rocking chair forward. When I take my hand off it, the chair rocks backwards. I repeat this demonstration a few times, and a predictable pattern of behavior becomes obvious. Forward motion is followed by backward motion. Then I take the bright red car and shoot it down the middle of the room. It usually comes to rest near the back of the room. The rocking chair is a good example of a structure that produces oscillation; the car is an example of advancement.

Next I take the car and place it in the seat of the rocking chair. I move the chair forward and then let it go. The result is like what happens in many organizations. No matter how much advancement has been accomplished, the organization still oscillates. In this type of organization, success eventually doesn't succeed.

Then I place the rocking chair on top of the car and push it. This is like an organization in which a resolving structure that produces advancement is dominant, even if it happens to contain some oscillating behavior. In this type of organization, true progress can happen, and you can get where you want to go.

Although organizations want resolving behaviors that lead to advancement, too often they are plagued with chronic oscillating behavior. Just as in the movement of a rocking chair, once we move toward our goals, we appear to reach a crucial point in which something seems to move us away from where we want to be. Every step forward seems to cause a step back, and progress is eventually neutralized.

Why did our success eventually lead to difficulties? Why did opportunities turn into problems? Everyone has a plausible explanation, but these explanations serve to cloud the real *structural* issue. Finger pointing may become a popular pastime as people attempt to decide why growth led to downsizing. Was it poor planning or bad leadership by senior management? Was it poor execution by the rank and file? Was it the economy? Competition from abroad? The cost of labor? Unimaginative research and development? A weak marketing strategy? Any or all of these factors might be present as symptoms, but they are not the cause. The question of what causes these symptoms is rarely asked. The answer may be found in the second inescapable law of organizational structure.

THE SECOND LAW OF ORGANIZATIONAL STRUCTURE

> **In organizations that oscillate, success is neutralized.**
>
> **In organizations that advance, success succeeds.**

Neutralizing Success in an Organization

In an oscillating organizational pattern, individuals, teams, departments, and divisions may create success, but does their success succeed overall? Often the answer is no; the organization is like my daughter's car, sitting in a rocking chair spinning its wheels.

Success in one department can cause difficulties in other parts of the organization. Increased sales can strain manufacturing capacity. New products can confuse buyers and lead to instability in established markets. Reinvestment can lead to declining stock market performance.

Structural consultant Chloe Cox, principal of the British firm Chloe Cox Consultants, has described success leading to failure as a chronic behavior that she and her colleagues repeatedly confront:

> In the past we helped many teams accomplish their goals on time and within budget. But six months after the big success, and celebratory Champagne, the accomplishments caused dilemmas in other parts of the organization. As a company, we decided to only do project planning or team development if we could be involved with the overall structure of the organization, or if the organization was well structured from the start. Otherwise, it is a waste of the client's money and our time.

Oscillation Camouflaged as Success

Success can camouflage oscillation, because success is rewarded whether or not an organization is governed by structural oscillation or advancement. Almost universally, success is seen as a good thing, something we would like repeated again and again. It is easy for people in an oscillating organization to focus on individual pockets of success and miss the overall nullification of success. Various factors, such as bonuses, promotions, increased authority, and higher salaries are the rewards of success, whether or not success ultimately succeeds.

Success disguises oscillation, because for many organizations some limited progress is made in spite of the oscillation. Small degrees of growth are squeezed out of the situation as people toil against the forces in play. Two steps forward, and one-and-three-quarter steps back does represent a type of movement. But at what cost?

In a rocking chair, oscillating behavior is a wonderful thing. But in an organization, oscillating behavior works against the aims of the enterprise. Too often the organization is blind to the consistent pattern of behavior that is working against its best efforts.

Success also disguises oscillation, because oscillating movement can take place over a long period of time, even years. When oscillation is slow, it is not obvious that a structural pattern is in play. The shorter time frame is filled with confronting events that seem to call for reactions or responses. Our focus is drawn to the immediate demands of the circumstances. This isn't wrong. When difficulties dominate the scene, our natural human instinct is to address them.

But if we only address symptoms, we become distracted from their causes. True change on the structural level is then unlikely. If problem solving and crisis intervention are chronic in the managerial process, long-range building becomes unlikely. In crisis intervention, the thinking goes that if we take corrective action we have solved the problem. But a flurry of activity hides what is really going on. We are deceived by temporary fixes. Later the same type of problem recurs, or a new problem arises out of the ashes of a previous solution—one we had thought to be completely successful.

Another reason why oscillating patterns of behavior are hard to see over long periods of time is that at least half the time is spent moving in the direction the organization wants to go. It seems that progress has been achieved, and everyone congratulates each other. Nevertheless, in such a pattern, *because* of success, difficulties are bound to happen. *In an oscillating pattern, movement in one direction will precipitate eventual movement in the other direction.* If a rocking chair moves forward, it must move back.

In an oscillating pattern our success can fool us, and then the eventual difficulties confound us. During their periods of growth, the IBMs, the GMs, the DECs of the world seemed to enjoy unending success. How were they to know they were subject to oscillation? When the cycle changed, profits declined and markets weakened. Those in senior positions were vilified as if they had caused the problems. Had they? Or were they, too, the victims of an oscillating structure in which past success was bound to lead to future decline? Even leaders can be victims of an inadequate structure.

These trends could have been predicted and prevented *if the peo-*

ple involved in those organizations understood the inherent structures in play.

The second law of organizational structure—success is neutralized when an organization oscillates, and succeeds when it advances—will always be in force, and what looks like success can be neutralized as soon as there is a reversal in the oscillating pattern. As the pendulum shifts, and some of these companies begin to succeed again, we are left with a question: Have they truly shifted to structural advancement, or are they simply setting up their next major decline?

How can an organization move from structural oscillation to structural advancement? How can success truly succeed? These are important questions that we can begin to answer by understanding the nature of structure. This is the focus of Chapter 2.

Quick Review

- Organizations follow inescapable structural laws.

- Understanding these laws will enable us to understand why organizations behave the way they do, and how we can redesign them to perform the way we want.

- The first law of organizational structure is: **Organizations either oscillate or advance.**

- Advancement means moving from where we are to where we want to be. Oscillation means moving from where we are toward where we want to be, but then moving back to the original position.

- The second law of organizational structure is: **In organizations that oscillate, success is neutralized. In ones that advance, success succeeds.**

- When success succeeds, one success breeds a chain of further successes. When success is neutralized, success is short-term or ephemeral.

- Since oscillating movement can take place over a long period of time, and some of that time the organization is moving in the direction it wants to go, oscillating patterns are often hard to observe.

- Organizations are often structured inadvertently, as smaller systems grow into larger systems, and management is fragmented. This unplanned arrangement almost always leads to structural oscillation.

- Understanding the nature of structure is essential for an organization to redesign itself so that it can move from oscillation to advancement.

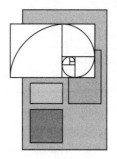

CHAPTER 2

Structure
The Power and the Beauty

Within every organization there are dominating forces that vie for influence and control of the company's direction. The impact that these forces have on each other and on the organization as a whole is not usually apparent to even the most knowledgeable people within the company. One primary reason is that little time is spent learning how the organization functions from a structural point of view. By discovering dominant forces in play that cause an organization to advance or oscillate, we can achieve a critical understanding of how the structure really operates.

Much of this chapter explores the topic of structure outside the context of organizations. Once we develop some background in its principles, we can better understand why structure is such an important area of concern for the organization, and how the organization, like the rest of nature, is influenced by structural principles.

Structure
Defining Structure

What structure is can best be understood by first discussing what it is not, then showing the power of structure, the tradition of structural thinking, and finally the meaning of structures within structural dynamics. When they hear the word *structure*, most organizational people think of boxes on charts. The term has been used for years to describe simple reporting relationships. But the term has been used inaccurately. Who reports to whom does not tell us anything about the structural dynamics that drive an organization to perform and behave as it does. If the real structure is not pondered, explored, and penetrated when designing the organization, it may never be understood.

People often think of structure as static, fixed, or stationary. Images that come to mind are girders, bridges, walls, or monuments. While we might think of these structures as immovable and rigid, they are far from static—although, if they work as designed, they will seem stationary. To create stability, the structure must contain innumerable dynamic relationships that produce balance, strength, and solidity. Structure is a dynamism that propels movement, change, transformation, and fluctuation. *When we think of structure as dynamic rather than static, we are closer to comprehending its nature.*

The study of structure teaches us how change can and must occur, and where it will land—in other words, what are the consequences of change, and what are the causes of these consequences. For example, knowing the structure of a skyscraper tells us how it will perform in a hurricane or earthquake, and why it will behave that way. By understanding the structure of a screenplay, we can predict what people will experience in various parts of the story, and make the film with that understanding.

Nowhere is the subject of *predictable* change more relevant than within our organizations. The valiant effort for organizational change over the past twenty-plus years testifies to the profound desire for something better than we have. But failure in the majority of these efforts reveals a hard truth: The dynamics of change were not well understood, and therefore, not able to be applied.

The Power of Structure

Structure has its own beauty, its own integrity, its own purpose, its own principles, its own inherent rhythm and texture and continuity.

That's not all, however. *Structure may also be accurately under-*

stood as a power. As a power, it dominates our lives and organizations through its ability to profoundly determine outcomes. No matter how well-intentioned, smart, visionary, open, or savvy we are, change will not succeed if the underlying structure we are in does not support it.

If the structure *does* support it, the probability of success is increased greatly.

But structure is often hard to see. We have not been trained to think structurally so, for the most part, the structures in our lives and organizations are invisible. The consequences of structure, however, are acutely visible in the circumstances in which we find ourselves—underfunded projects that lack full support of the organization, unclear strategies, tactics that compete against each other, compensation systems that reward values opposite the ones espoused, major direction of the organization changing every few years, proclamations that mean little in the daily running of the company, and so on. All of these are consequences of structure.

If we fail to understand the powerful causal nature of structure, we are less able to create new and desired outcomes. By understanding structure, we are well positioned to serve our highest aspirations and deepest values.

The Structuralist Tradition

The study of structure has a long tradition in the arts, sciences, and engineering. Those who are particularly interested in the subject are called *structuralists*. Beethoven was a structuralist, as was Bach, Mozart and Schoenberg. Other structuralists include Steven Spielberg, Frank Lloyd Wright, Robert Frost, William Shakespeare, and Dante. For composers, playwrights, filmmakers, architects, graphic artists, or mathematicians, the subject of structure is not an intellectual luxury; it is their stock in trade. It would be impossible for these people to produce their work if they did not have a firm grasp of structural principles.

Many structuralists were trained in music or mathematics—probably the most purely structural languages there are. In the world of management, the work of the great thinkers Peter Drucker and W. Edwards Deming are filled with structural insights. Both had backgrounds in music. Drucker considered becoming a professional musician before he became interested in management issues. Deming, a statistician, was also a composer.

Because most people have not been trained in structural principles, they are hardly aware that such a topic exists. But, when we begin to consider and study structural principles, we open ourselves to a new world of understanding as to why organizations do what they do. Rather than react or respond unproductively to unwanted symptoms, we can redesign the organization's underlying structure, assuring that it will perform the way we want it to.

The Field of Structural Dynamics

The work I have been developing over the past twenty years is called *structural dynamics*; it is the study of how structure works and what kind of impact it has. The field is still young, but several revolutionary discoveries have been made that help us rethink many basic assumptions built into our culture—including many of the basic popular assumptions about organizations.

Of course, the term *structure* has been used in a variety of contexts. Within structural dynamics, the term has a technically exact meaning:

> **Structure is an entity formed by the influence
> the parts have on each other and on the whole.**

The first notion included within this definition is that structure is an *entity*. That is to say, structure has a totality to it, a singleness. Structure has integrity and unity.

While an organization has a totality, we usually don't think about it that way. Ordinarily, we think about the parts as parts: teams, departments, functions, products, personalities, strategies, policies, distribution systems, customers, processes, competing interests, activities, leadership, and so on. While these elements do exist, they do not exist in a vacuum. Many individual factors combine to form the organization.

The second notion within the definition of structure implies parts—the existence of individual *elements*; the third notion is the nature of the *relationship* they form when combined. For a relationship to be structural, the elements must influence each other. Each element must have impact on the others.

Structure is:
- ***an entity***
- ***made up of individual elements***
- ***that impact each other by the relationships they form***

It would be impossible to have a structure if we did not have individual elements. But individual elements do not a structure make. A collection of "stuff" such as stamps, or butterflies, or books, has a sense of unity. However, the inclusion or exclusion of any one stamp would not affect the behavior of the other stamps. The relationship is not a structural relationship because the parts do not have an impact on each other.

If we thought of an organization as only a collection of parts, we would not understand the significance or function that the parts had within its structural unity.

And yet the organization is a structure, whether we recognize it or not. As its various elements combine, affecting each other, we are confronted by their structural dynamics.

Not *all* parts of the organization form structural relationships, however. And not *all* structural relationships are of equal importance. This makes it a bit harder to see what the structural elements are, which sets of relationships are dominant, and which elements are not structural at all. All things not being equal, the parts in relationship to each other must be explored with a discerning eye. The structure is there—it's only a question of perceiving it.

STRUCTURAL DYNAMICS AND SYSTEMS THINKING: CLOSE COUSINS

My friend and colleague Peter Senge has named systems thinking as one of the essential ingredients of the learning organization in his wildly popular book *The Fifth Discipline*. Systems thinking and structural dynamics are two disciplines that are exceedingly compatible, containing many overlapping principles and parallel inclinations. Both encourage people to think in terms of wholes rather than in fragmented parts. Both enable people to understand networks of relationships as an intrinsic property of cause and effect. Both enable people to shift their viewpoint from bouts of tunnel vision to a wider understanding of the interconnectedness of events to each other over time. Both encourage organizational learning by enabling people to co-explore the complex issues they face. These are just some of the advantages shared by systems thinking and structural dynamics.

But there are important differences between systems thinking and structural dynamics. Some of them are technical and some are philosophical. It is important to know that systems thinking is *not* structural dynamics, and structural dynamics is *not* systems thinking. To better appreciate each discipline, it is best not to attempt to fuse them as if they were different aspects of the same understanding.

Sometimes a systems approach can be better than a structural approach in understanding complexity, for example, when using the tools of causal loop mapping, computer modeling, and diagnostic archetyping. Sometimes a structural approach is better in understanding and describing patterns of cause and effect, and trends of organizational performance. Structural dynamics is superior as an organizational design tool for business strategy and management implementation. Since both disciplines exist, we can utilize the best of each.

One of the technical differences between structural dynamics and systems thinking is found in the central mechanism used in each approach. In structural dynamics, it is *tension-resolution* (discussed in the next section). In systems thinking, as expressed in the work on system dynamics by MIT's Jay Forrester and his colleagues, it is the *feedback loop*.

In its attempt to understand complex systems, system dynamics uses two types of feedback loops. These are called positive and negative feedback, or growth and balancing loops. A growth loop reinforces direction, a balancing loop limits direction and is self-regulating.

A growth loop produces the economic principle of increasing returns in which "the more you have, the more you get." Your bank account earns interest, which is added to your capital, which then earns more interest.

While, with a growth loop, more begets more and less begets less, a balance loop regulates and limits growth by comparing a fixed goal with actual variances. The thermostat is set to a fixed goal—the desired temperature. When the temperature in the room falls below that goal, the thermostat turns the furnace on, and it continues to heat the room until the temperature rises above the thermostat setting. At that point, the thermostat turns off the furnace.

Feedback loops combine with other feedback loops to form complex systems. System dynamics use feedback loops as a tool in analyzing and understanding complexity within social, economic, ecological, and organizational systems, and many organizations are beginning to use loop diagrams to explore critical issues they face.[1]

The feedback loop is the basic unit of system dynamics, as words are to language, or numbers are to mathematics. Within structural dynamics *tension-resolution* is the basic unit.

Structural Tension

The tension-resolution system is the root of structure. To understand tension, let us first illustrate the basic principles of tension using a non-organizational example, then explore structural axioms that explain some of the basic tenets of structural dynamics, and finally discuss tension within an organization.

The Basics of Tension

Tension is formed by discrepancy, or the difference between one thing and another.

A simple example of a tension is thirst. There is a discrepancy between how much liquid the body needs and how much it actually has at any moment. This discrepancy creates a tension that in turn produces a tendency for behavior toward action that ends the discrepancy. Thirst is resolved by drinking liquid until the body's actual state is the same as the body's desired state (see illustration at the top of the next page).

In this simple example, we can observe some of the most important principles about tension:

1. Tension is formed by a discrepancy between two elements.

2. Tension creates a tendency for movement.

3. Tension resolves when the discrepancy ends.

In structural dynamics, tension is the fundamental causal force.

---

[1] I recommend *The Fifth Discipline* and *The Fifth Discipline Fieldbook* by Peter Senge and colleagues, the books of Donella (Dana) Meadows, the writings of Jay Forrester, and the newsletter *The Systems Thinker* (Pegasus Communications, Cambridge, MA.) for those who are interested in exploring the subject.

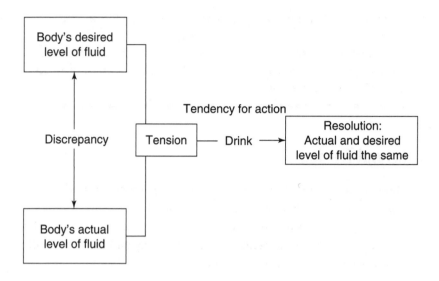

Once a tension is formed, it contains within it, a dynamic—the tendency to move from one condition to another. Tension possesses its own generative drive, which gives rise to an impetus to move away from the state of tension toward a resolution. Tension seeks resolution. Whenever a tension exists, it will strive for resolution.

Structural Axioms

Let's summarize and expand on what has been described so far about structure in the form of axioms. Axioms about structure are useful in understanding the principles that govern patterns of behaviors in general. In contrast, structural laws apply specifically to the behavior of organizations.

AXIOM 1

- **Structure is formed by relationships among elements.**

A college professor of mine once made the point in a colorful way. He said, "If you have one blob of paint on a canvas, you don't have structure. If you have two blobs, you do." Without relationship, there is no structure. In our example of thirst, the relationship between the body's desired level of fluid and its actual level are two elements that are in relationship with each other.

AXIOM 2

- **Structural relationships create tendencies for behavior.**

In a structural relationship, individual elements combine to form a dynamic that generates a tendency for change. A structural relationship does not exist as a static condition. Even stable conditions can be tracked back to preceding dynamic conditions that led to subsequent stability. The relationship between the body's desired amount of fluid and the actual amount creates particular tendencies for behavior (to drink when they are different, to stop drinking when they are the same).

AXIOM 3

- **The basic unit of structure is the tension-resolution system.**

The smallest denominator in a structural relationship is the single tension-resolution system. A single tension creates a generative dynamic force. Thirst is such a system.

AXIOM 4

- **Tension is produced by the discrepancy between two elements that are structurally connected.**

To form a tension, there must be two elements that are discrepant, or different. Differences imply similarities, because without a basis of similarities we would not be able to identify differences, and elements would merely be a juxtaposition of unrelated objects. The two elements that form a tension must have a basis of similarity that tie them together. Thirst is a tension formed by a discrepancy between amounts of water in the body. The similarity is water, the difference is the amount.

AXIOM 5

■ Once a tension exists, it generates a tendency to move toward resolution.

Tension creates a state of non-equilibrium. In our thirst example, the desired amount of water *is not equal* to the actual amount of water. When a state of non-equilibrium exists within a structure, the structure attempts to restore equilibrium. Thirst—the tension—generates a tendency to drink fluids, which resolves the state of non-equilibrium and ends the discrepancy within the system. By itself, equilibrium is neither good nor bad. The same can be said for states of non-equilibrium. Being thirsty or not being thirsty is neither good nor bad; it merely reflects the state of tension within the body's biological system.

As stated earlier, axioms apply to life in general. Let's now see how they can be applied to organizations.

Tension Within Organizations

Tension is a key element of organizational competence. But the word *tension* can have overtones of unpleasantness, since the term also is used to describe emotional stress and anxiety. Our use of the term is technical rather than descriptive. When we refer to tension, we are talking about a dynamic force rather than a state of anguish. Ironically, an organization that is "under a lot of tension" is probably an organization in which the tensions are not well-structured.

In all of our business and managerial design work, our clients create *structural tension*,[2] in which desired results are positioned in relationship to the actual state as in the accompanying illustration.

This illustration (on the next page) can be explained using the axioms we have discussed. There is a structural relationship between the actual state (where we are) and the desired state (where we want

---

[2]*Structural tension* is the term I have given this particular structural relationship. Some who have adopted my work have called this "creative tension." The term *creative* is misleading, because *creative* means departure from the norm. If anything, we would want this structure to become the norm in our organizations. Since I discovered and first named this concept, I prefer people to call it structural tension, which properly emphasizes the structural nature of the relationship.

Structural Tension

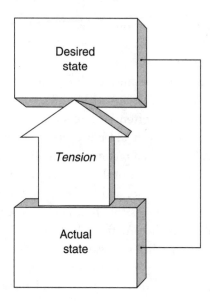

to be). The difference between these two conditions, the discrepancy, creates a tension. This tension generates a tendency to move from the actual state to the desired state—our goals. The organization will thus resolve the non-equilibrium between the actual and desired states by achieving its goals.

Knowing that establishing tension will tend to resolve in the direction of our chosen goals, organizations can use a structural approach strategically to orchestrate states of non-equilibrium. In the beginning of building a project, strategy, tactic, or goal, a state of non-equilibrium is established between the desired state (the finished product, the release date, the percentage of market share) and the current state (the current state of the product, the current date in relationship to the release date, the current percentage of market share).

When we begin to aim tension toward desired results, we greatly increase the chance of success. Within management strategy, an organization that establishes tension, or states of non-equilibrium, is able to let structure support it. The organization is working with, rather than against, the forces in play. Once we establish structural tension, we are able to develop and implement action strategies, and the organization is able to coordinate its efforts toward the desired outcomes.

Misperceptions

Because structural tension is easy to articulate and easy to understand superficially, it is also easy to ignore or misinterpret. Since I first introduced structural tension over fifteen years ago, it has been adopted by many companies, been referred to in many books and articles, and been talked about within all kinds of management circles. Unfortunately, it has often lost something in the "translation." Some who attempted to use it did not understand its structural basis, and merely thought of it as a metaphor or managerial device. When structural tension is taken out of the context of structural dynamics, it can seem trivial or simplistic, and its fantastic power cannot be realized.

Structural tension is much easier to describe conceptually than it is to apply in reality. At first blush it can sound like simple common sense: Know what you want, know what you have, take actions to move from where you are to where you want to be. But when we begin to apply structural tension—to implement it well—what seemed simple begins to demand enormous rigor and discipline.

The first hurdle is that of determining desired outcomes. Being able to define precisely what they want is rare among management groups, who don't always agree but don't always know that they don't agree. The desired outcomes do not always fit within the grand strategy of the company. In fact, more often than not, we have seen teams create goals irrelevant to the organization's business strategy: for example, a goal of increasing the number of new products, when the business strategy targets a narrow product range for greater market penetration; or developing additional services that add to the price of a product, which makes it less competitive.

Without a vision of a clear end result, it is impossible to create structural tension. We will explore constructing highly workable end results in Part 3 of this book.

Then we come to the skill of defining reality precisely: Where are we in relationship to our goals? This aspect of establishing the actual state in relation to the desired state requires that management groups observe reality with a much higher level of objectivity than is usual. Why is defining current reality so hard? Because we have been trained to see the world through the lens of our theories, experiences, ideals, worldviews, opinions, and speculations. These lenses can distort reality, which will weaken or even destroy structural tension. Observing reality objectively is another discipline we will explore in Part 3.

Once we establish structural tension by defining a desired end result and defining its current reality, we are ready to think about action plans—the actions that will resolve the tension between the points of discrepancy and move us toward our goals.

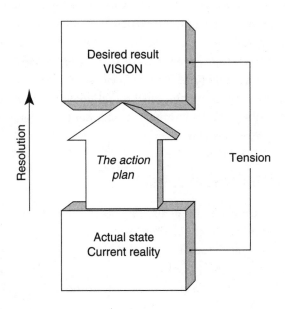

What are the steps we must take in moving from here to there? Within the form of structural tension, highly effective and practical plans can be tailor-made. But making these plans is not simply "filling in the gap" as I have sometimes heard it erroneously described. A gap suggests an empty space between something and something else. Instead of an empty space (the absence of something) there is a tension (the presence of a dynamic force). Tension, as a dynamic force, seeks resolution. One way we begin to resolve the tension is by constructing action plans. Another way is by implementing these plans.

Those who talk of "gaps" are not aware of how tangible and powerful tension is, and what a dynamic force it represents. They do not understand it as a *structure*. As a structure, not only can it produce a high level of order within management systems, but it also contains its own generative power.

When real structural tension is established and managed, those involved do not have to manipulate an uncooperative system through force and conflict. Instead energy is generated from the system, which then enables people to take advantage of the tension. Over time momentum develops, and conditions become easier than they would be otherwise. Then success breeds further success, and the organization advances.

Organizations that advance have structural tension as their dominant underlying structure. The behaviors that we observe in these companies are impressive: organizational goals are interrelated; reality is seen and reported accurately; adjustments to plans become easier; learning becomes the norm.

The Interrelationship of Goals

Every organization has its goals, but do the members of the organization know and understand the *function* of the major goals they are attempting to create? Too often, goals in one department remain uncoordinated with the goals of other departments. Goals created on local levels of the organization may have little to do with goals created on the corporate level. Dr. Jay Merluzzi, director of immunological diseases for Boehringer Ingelheim, has noted this point when describing how young scientists who first come to industry often fail to match scientific goals with organizational goals:

> Many young scientists who come to industry find themselves as managers of laboratories and groups. In most cases, scientists have the talent, intellectual capability and knowledge to accomplish technical goals. But sometimes the science gets clouded . . . by a lack of wisdom. I have found that scientists can easily define the end-result of a scientific goal but they are not as adept at seeing the organizational goals that are needed to reach the technical target. As a technical/professional manager, I have found that setting up strong structural tension around well-defined organizational goals results in movement technically where there was little or none before. It is extremely effective.

In an organization built on structural tension, goals have a special function—they are the *prime organizing principles* of the organization. *Every* action taken is linked to goals that are linked to other related, more senior, goals. From the overall purpose of the organization, to its business strategy, management strategy, and local level, all goals are related.

The Relatedness of Goals

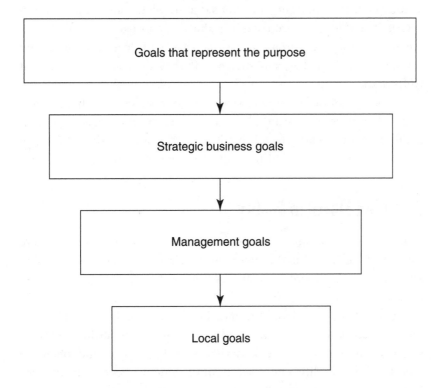

Contrast this relatedness of goals to the non-relational approach most organizations take. Goals are created by departments or teams, which are guided by the general mandates that they are given. People are asked to form their own goals, but too often they are not told the context in which these goals must exist. Consequently, they construct goals in a vacuum. Because they have an inadequate understanding of the company's business direction, they must rely on their local perception, which can be limited.

Goals conceived from a local point of view do not always mesh with goals other members of the organization have created. Goals may clash, setting up a situation where various groups must fight it out for adequate resources in order to do their jobs. Eventually, some win and some lose in a "survival of the fittest," goal-eat-goal world. What is absent is a true organizing principle that ties all efforts together.

In an organization designed to advance, the approach toward goal setting is targeted and relational. Every goal is the child of a parent goal, right up to the organization's purpose. Therefore each goal has a strategic function. In organizations that oscillate, one common characteristic is that goals are used in a shotgun approach toward accomplishment. Such organizations assume that, with legions of goals and actions occurring, they will succeed. If they do enough, some of it will stick.

Most organizations are not rich enough to succeed at that game— and if they were, they would be at a definite disadvantage from competitors who were structured to advance. Any success that a shotgun approach may achieve will be neutralized in an oscillating structure.

Becoming Fluent in Reality

It is not enough to have well-organized goals. We need to know where we are in relationship to these goals. Organizations structured to advance become fluent in reality as it is, and as it changes. They are able to track *current* reality.

In most organizations, the members distort reality. Mistakes are hidden, success is exaggerated, and people ignore the obvious. Reward systems can reinforce the behavior of hiding facts, and objective reports about reality can lead to punishment. People avoid confrontations by managing news so that reality is portrayed as more agreeable than it is.

Sometimes reality is filled with pain, disappointment, and frustration. Sometimes it proves that our firm beliefs do not hold up to scrutiny. Sometimes reality can seem confusing. But, *if we are to establish real structural tension, the current state of reality in relationship to the desired state must be well known and articulated.*

Reality is an acquired taste. At first it can seem bitter or cold, but with more exposure, reality moves from something we tolerate to something we appreciate. As Robert Frost said, "Anything more than the truth, would have been too weak."

The Ease of Adjustments

In organizations in which structural tension is dominant, people can be accurate and objective about reality, and they can tell each other what they see. They explore differences of opinion and observation, and they help each other clarify the actual state in relation to the desired state. When this is the case, strategies and action plans can be evaluated and adjusted based on true learning, rather than reactions against conflicts and problems.

In organizations structured to advance, actions *lead* to evaluations, which *lead* to adjustments, which *lead* to other actions. True innovation is more likely than ever before, as is the refined use of conventional methods and common processes.

Any process is only as good as the results it produces. Only when we understand just what the process needs to accomplish can we truly reinvent and redesign it. John Teti, vice-chairman of the La France Corporation (a medium-sized manufacturing company that is a supplier for Hewlett-Packard, Ford Motors, Tandy, and others) put it like this:

> I don't think our process planning was very efficient when we started to use a structural approach. But when we started applying it, we didn't say anything to anyone. We didn't give it any grand introduction. We just started using it, and what it did immediately was eliminate a lot of talk about irrelevant things. When we started talking about what any particular goal was, and clarified reality, our planning time was cut by a third.

And La France's executive vice-president George Barrar said:

> By using a structural approach, we got an awful lot of insights into the business that we wouldn't normally have gotten. I think from a process planning standpoint one of the big improvements is [that] before we did a lot of fluff.

Management trends that promote process redesign, such as business process reengineering, often lose their value as they lose their functional reason to produce specific or general results. When any management process comes into vogue, the fad makes it easy for people to forget the point of the actions they are taking. This often happens when people search for the best practices and for improved efficiency without tying these activities to their specific goals. What does the process serve? There is nothing wrong with wanting better processes or studying the methods others have used. But too often people forget the fundamental purpose of any process—the result it serves.

We can only measure the actual efficiency of a process within the context of our goals. Without a clear relationship between a goal and its current reality, how could we know if the changes in process really worked?

Putting Learning into Practice

In an organization that advances, people are better able to learn and they can put that learning into practice immediately. They are less bureaucratic, more flexible, and more practical than those in most other organizations. In addition, learning continues to take place once a project is complete, owing to a thoughtful evaluation process. And the learning is not lost; it is put into practice in subsequent projects and enterprises.

Structural tension becomes the fundamental organizing force governing the organization. As La France's John Teti put it, "People get sensitized to structural tension, and they recognize what works and what doesn't work. The logic never leaves them. The actions they take are never arbitrary. They can learn right away, and help each other learn too."

John Wolverton, an internal structural consultant and program manager at the United States Air Force's Wright Laboratory, sees the structural approach, and especially structural tension, as the key factor in expanding managerial greatness across the organization:

> I've had the privilege of working with only a few really great managers in my life. What fascinated me the most was their ability to consistently produce results, no matter what the issues were. I've been looking most of my life for that principle or key process they possessed that others didn't. Now, based on my

work with the structural approach, it is obvious what the key is. It is structural tension. I can't imagine managing a project any other way now.

Katherine Freeman, Director of Riverside Methodist Hospital's Alcohol and Drug Dependency department, reports that the use of the structural approach in her organization has led to a new pattern of success:

> After we did our first training in the structural approach back in 1993, we were able to create remarkable results. Ten or twelve years prior to that, director after director had the same issues and had really never much achieved any end results that they wanted, certainly never had any financial results. There was a lot of talk about management strategy, but it wasn't working.
>
> Over a three year period we completely restructured the clinical program using structural tension, and aligning all the pieces. We ended up last year with better patient outcomes, less recidivism than ever before and made the strongest and only contribution to the bottom line in the history of the department. And we ended up with incredibly high morale. To the physicians in behavioral health, this was a miracle. They started to want to know what happened in our department that caused our success.

Structural tension produces resolving behavior that leads to structural advancement, and if all you take away from this book is a knowledge of how to create structural tension, you will be faring very well indeed. However, you would not be able to understand or change what is going on when an oscillating structure is in play. What causes organizations to oscillate? This is a question we will answer in the next few chapters.

Quick Review

- Structure is an entity that is made up of individual elements that are interrelated.

- To understand how a structure works, relationships between elements and how each individual element affects the others must be discovered and understood.

- Structural tension—the desired state in relation to the actual state—is the key ingredient in organizations that advance.

- Once a tension exists, it creates a tendency to move toward resolution. The basic unit of structure is the tension-resolution system.

- Interrelated goals are the primary organizing principle within structural tension.

- It takes rigor and discipline to design structural tension into an organization.

- Structural tension produces advancement in an organization because of the organizational behaviors that it promotes: goals are interrelated, reality is seen objectively, adjustments to plans and organizational learning become the norm.

- Axiom 1: **Structure is formed by relationships among elements.**

- Axiom 2: **Structural relationships create tendencies for behavior.**

- Axiom 3: **The basic unit of structure is the tension-resolution system.**

- Axiom 4: **Tension is produced by the discrepancy between two elements that are structurally connected.**

- Axiom 5: **Once a tension exists, it generates a tendency to move toward resolution.**

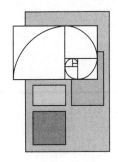

CHAPTER 3

Structural Conflict
Why Organizations Oscillate

Most organizations have many oscillating patterns that recycle regularly. Decision making can move from tightly centralized control, in which a few people in senior management positions make all major decisions, to decentralized control, in which many people from the organization are given responsibility to make major decisions. Such localized decision making may then be re-centralized if results are not as desired by management.

Members of an organization may be encouraged to take independent action, then required to march in close step with senior leadership, only to be asked to act independently again.

The financial direction of the organization can move from an emphasis on cost-cutting, to investment, back to cost-cutting.

The company as a whole can move from an inventive mode, to an emphasis on convention, back to innovation.

Organizations expand, then downsize, then expand once again.

In these types of oscillating patterns, the organization squanders money, time, resources, intellectual capital, morale, reputation, and market share.

No one wants these oscillating patterns, so why do they exist? They exist because of a fundamental structural mechanism I have termed *structural conflict*. This chapter discusses structural conflicts and how they produce oscillation.

The Form of Structural Conflict

While structural tension is produced by a simple tension-resolution system, structural conflict results from a more complex structural arrangement: two competing tension-resolution systems based on two competing goals. When an organization oscillates, structural conflict is in play.

First, let's study how the structure works in a simple non-organizational example.

Hunger produces a tension that is resolved by eating:

But if we are overweight (our actual weight is discrepant with our desired weight) we may form another tension resolution system:

As each system moves toward its own resolution, it competes with the conflicting system. First, the dominant tension is hunger. In order to resolve that tension, we eat:

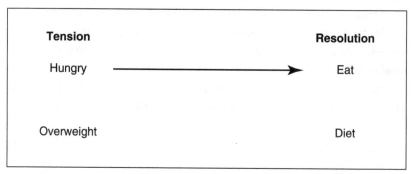

Once we have eaten, our hunger subsides but our weight goes up. The amount we weigh is discrepant with the amount we want to weigh. This discrepancy then becomes the more pronounced tension:

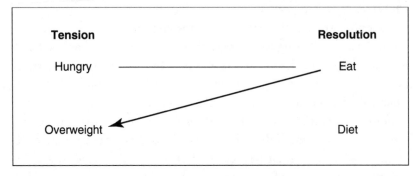

In order to resolve this tension, we may eat less, or skip meals:

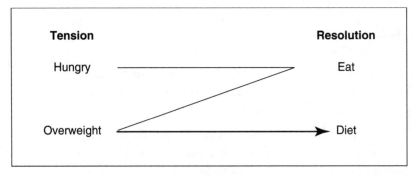

We may lose some pounds and begin to feel better about our weight. But the body reacts to reduction of fat and protein by sending a starvation warning, triggering the brain's appestat. This causes an increasing discrepancy between the body's desired amount of food and actual amount of food. Hunger once again becomes the bigger tension as the brain relays the message: "Eat! Eat! Eat!"

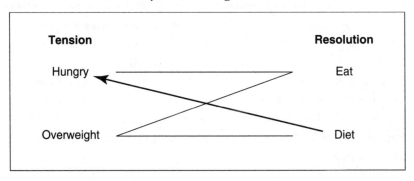

The shift of dominance between the first and second tension-resolution system produces a predictable pattern of behavior. Hunger leads to eating, which leads to weight gain, which leads to dieting, which leads to hunger.

Movement from the first tension-resolution system to the second, produces an oscillating *behavior* familiar to anyone who has tried dieting and failed. Yet the *structure* causing the failure is not obvious. People who experience this cycle fear they are to blame for being weak-willed or lacking discipline. They do not realize that, within this structure, no amount of heightened resolve will work. Every time they force themselves into a diet, the structure compensates for any movement, so eventually their best efforts fail. They are up against a structure that is inadequate for the behavior they desire. This example illustrates two additional structural axioms.

AXIOM 6

■ Structural conflict exists when two tension-resolution systems within the same structure have points of resolution that are mutually exclusive.

Each system creates its own tendency—to move toward its own resolution. But as each system resolves, the tension in the competing system increases.

AXIOM 7

■ Structural conflicts produce oscillating behavior.

As one competing tension-resolution system moves toward resolution, the other tension-resolution system becomes dominant. Less tension in one leads to more tension in the other. This change produces a *shift of dominance*, but this shift is not permanent. Once the new higher tension begins to move toward its resolution, there is another shift of dominance back to the original, creating an oscillating pattern, as shown in the accompanying illustration at the top of the next page.

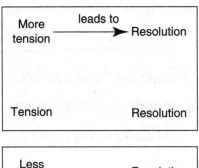

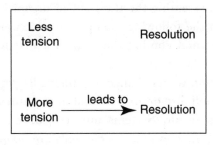

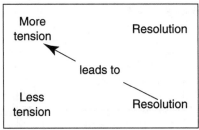

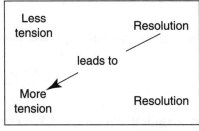

The reason for oscillation is found in this next axiom.

AXIOM 8

■ **Movement in one direction of a structural conflict will precipitate compensating movement in the other direction.**

Now let's apply the form of structural conflict to an organization.

THE THIRD LAW OF ORGANIZATIONAL STRUCTURE

> # When structural conflicts dominate an organization, oscillation will result.

Oscillation

We have asked why organizations oscillate. We can begin to answer this question by presenting the third law of organizational structure. It is illustrated in the following example, in which an organization is trapped in a structural conflict that causes it first to embrace, then reject, change.

The organization wants change to improve its performance, avoid stagnation, and capitalize on its potential. It institutes a program, and changes begin to occur. Systems are reorganized, cross-discipline teams are formed, new evaluation methods are adopted, and people move to new positions.

However, as the changes take place, they bring with them a degree of instability and discontinuity. Work becomes harder to accomplish as familiar lines of communication disappear. People begin to feel unsure of what is expected of them, what they need to do to fulfill the new mandates, and who is now in charge. Even though new policies and principles are clearly stated, actual conditions seem quite different from the ideals being expressed. In light of all the upheaval, people begin to long for continuity, and eventually this becomes a dominant tension.

This tension is resolved by rejecting change. People may bypass new lines of authority or ignore new policies. Support for the changes weakens as factions develop. The change effort is subtly undermined, and morale dips.

At this point in the cycle, the organization has returned to business as usual, and the change effort is recognized as a failure. But a return to the old ways brings its own set of problems. Growth is limited, creativity restrained, and improvement stifled. After a time of living with stagnation, new calls for change fill the air.

Over periods of years, the company cycles through several shifts from change to continuity. Each effort at change grows out of limitation and stagnation; each move back to the status quo comes from discontinuity that the change efforts have brought.

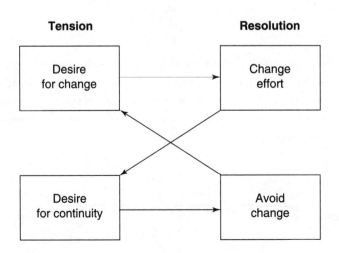

Many organizations are subject to this structure without understanding the dynamics in play. Change is resisted, but so is stagnation. Continuity and change seem in a constant, unwinnable battle with each other. People often experience the frustration of neither losing nor gaining ground. Or perhaps every new change effort—for even the simplest advancements—requires mounting an enormous campaign. After a while, members of the organization may begin to wonder if change is worth the trouble.

Let's look more closely at the actual causes of these types of shifts. To demonstrate the dynamic nature of competing tension-resolution systems, imagine a rubber band tied around us as we attempt to resolve one of the tension-resolution systems: change.

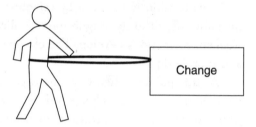

Now imagine another rubber band, tied around us, but connected to our other desired state: continuity.

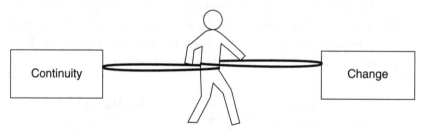

As we move toward the first of our goals—change—the tension-resolution system begins to resolve and change occurs. As it does, what is happening to the other tension-resolution system, the rubber band connected to continuity? It is stretching, so tension in that system is increasing.

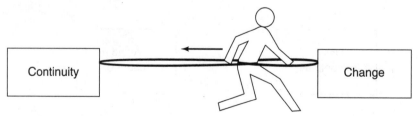

Now, where is it easier for us to move? Where is the path of least resistance? Obviously it is away from the goal of change and toward the goal of continuity.

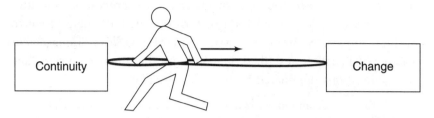

But as soon as the *continuity* rubber band begins to resolve, the *change* rubber band begins to stretch. Its tension is increasing. Where is it now easier for us to move? Back toward *change*—again.

Oscillation between the theme of change and the theme of continuity repeats itself again and again. When change is addressed, desire for continuity gradually increases until it becomes the dominant theme. People act to restore the organization's sense of continuity. But the pendulum shifts yet again, and people begin to hope for change to support growth and expansion of the enterprise.

These shifts may take years to happen—so slowly that it is hard to observe a predictable pattern. This oscillating pattern can be disguised as other issues burst on the scene and demand attention, and events seem to rise out of the immediate situation. However, the real cause of these conditions will not be found in the issues, events or personnel, but in the structure which is inadequate for change, growth or continuity.

Most often, change attempts do not succeed. Is this because change, by its nature, is resisted? Common wisdom says change is hard. But is it, when change is well motivated? I don't personally know anyone who would go back to a typewriter after using a word processor. Perhaps there is the rugged individualist, a self-styled Hemingway, somewhere who prefers to bang away on an old IBM electric or a mechanical Remington. But, if such a being exists, he or she would be the exception to the rule. Some change happens easily, overnight, and permanently. Organizational complexity notwithstanding, change can happen when the underlying structure supports it. But when the dominant structure of an organization is structural conflict, and oscillation is the resulting pattern of behavior, then the most successful change program will lose its momentum and eventually be neutralized.

The management literature had been filled with success stories about TQM, or reengineering, or other change processes. But after all the years of success stories a pattern of failed attempts began to surface. Robert S. Kaufman, writing in MIT's *Sloan Management Review* (Fall, 1992) described the condition that many managers face in organizations dominated by structural oscillation:

> Your predicament as manager of a manufacturing revival is common: After years of educating yourself in the concepts of just-in-time and employee involvement, you launched an ambitious program in your company. After achieving dramatic productivity gains, you were convinced you were on the road to success. But the gains turned out to be only temporary, and now you're less optimistic. Employees are devoting less time to the program. Like failed initiatives of the past, it is being referred to with that terminal phrase, "just another program."
>
> You have tried all you can think of to revive the program, with little success. You are beginning to wonder whether you and your team have what it takes.

What Does the Structure Want?

This next point is important if we are to understand why structural conflict operates the way it does.

Let us pose this question: What does the structure want? In other words, what is the structure's goal?

The situation is this: Two tension-resolution systems are competing against each other. Each individual system has the local structural goal of resolving that system's tension. But it is impossible to resolve both systems simultaneously, because whenever we move toward resolution in one system, tension in the other system intensifies. A repeated shift of dominance from one system to the other produces oscillation. The structure cannot resolve both of the tension-resolution systems simultaneously because of an imbalance existing between the systems. Here is a key factor: *imbalance*. The structure wants to reduce the *imbalance*, to create a *balance* or *equilibrium* between the two tension-resolution systems between the two goals.

When I say the structure "wants" balance, I do not mean to imply that structure has a mind, a will of its own, a personality, or a vested interest in the outcome, anymore than gravity has. It is an impersonal fact of nature.

The structure wants *equilibrium*, but we want something that will produce *non-equilibrium*.

We may want change:

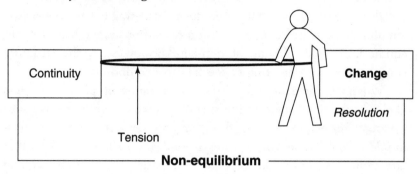

We may want continuity:

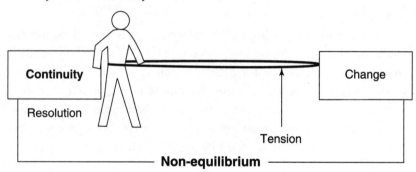

But the structure wants balance between the two competing tension-resolution systems, so that each tension equals the other:

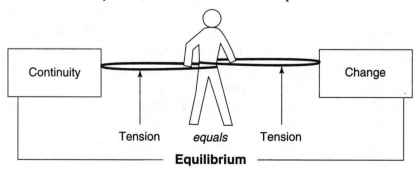

AXIOM 9

■ **Structure seeks equilibrium.**

Within this structural conflict, anytime we move toward *change*, equilibrium is lost. If we move toward *continuity*, the equilibrium is also lost. So, movement toward either side of the conflict sets up an imbalance. Structural conflicts produce oscillating behaviors because any shift in dominance in one tension-resolution system leads to non-equilibrium. Once a state of non-equilibrium exists, the structure compensates by attempting to reestablish equilibrium.

When we understand the structural dynamics in play, we are less likely to take sides, be it on the side of change or continuity, because we know movement in either direction only serves to widen the magnitude of oscillation, and creates a tendency to move in the other direction. But neither do we want to be stuck between change and continuity. Structural conflict, as we can see, is an inadequate structure in which to accomplish our purpose of successful change while maintaining adequate continuity.

The key to penetrating structural dynamics is to understand that states of non-equilibrium are forces in play. A state of non-equilibrium creates an impetus for action, which is a structural motivation to restore a state of equilibrium. As was said in Chapter 2, neither non-equilibrium nor equilibrium is good or bad. Some states of non-equilibrium manifest themselves as tensions that, like an archer's bow and arrow, can help us hit the targets at which we aim.

Structural Conflicts: Not Problems

Structural conflicts are not problems. They are simply inadequate structures to accomplish our ends. They are like rocking chairs, structures designed to oscillate. That's all they can do. If we found ourselves in a rocking chair, but we wanted to travel downtown, we would not attempt to "fix" our rocking chair by putting wheels on it, or by installing a motor, steering wheel, and brakes. We would move from the rocking chair to a car.

This analogy holds true for organizations. When we are confronted with inadequate structures, our temptation is to enter into a problem-solving mode.

We have been taught, when something is wrong, fix it. But fixing something ill-designed to begin with does little to help us achieve our aims. The fourth law of organizational structure reveals a profound insight: that organizations do not need fixing, they need to be redesigned.

THE FOURTH LAW OF ORGANIZATIONAL STRUCTURE

> ## An inadequate organizational structure cannot be fixed. But you can move from an inadequate structure to a suitable structure.

Fixing something means that we take what is there and repair it. Redesigning something means that we start from scratch and rethink the basic premises that guide us. Then, we can create new structures to accommodate our intentions, or use current ones if they prove themselves to be adequate for our purposes.

Just as we do not "fix" our rocking chair so that it will be a car, we cannot "fix" an oscillating organizational structure so that it will be a resolving one that advances.

Quick Review

• Unwanted oscillating patterns recycle regularly within most organizations.

• These patterns are caused by structural conflicts, structures in which two tension-resolution systems or two goals are competing against each other.

• When one tension-resolution moves toward resolution, the competing one's tension increases.

- Thus, movement in one direction of a structural conflict will precipitate compensating movement in the other direction.

- A structural conflict between two goals makes both goals difficult to accomplish.

- The third law of organizational structure is: **When structural conflicts dominate an organization, an organizational oscillation will result.**

- Structure has the goal of establishing equilibrium between competing goals. Within an organization, equilibrium is not necessarily desirable because it dampens the incentive to take action toward goals.

- States of non-equilibrium, however, give rise to movement that functions to restore equilibrium.

- Structural conflicts are not problems that can be fixed, they are merely inadequate structures that prevent advancement.

- The fourth law of organizational structure is: **An inadequate organizational structure cannot be fixed, but we can move from an inadequate to a suitable structure.**

- Axiom 6: **Structural conflict exists when two tension-resolution systems within the same structure have points of resolution that are mutually exclusive.**

- Axiom 7: **Structural conflicts produce oscillating behavior.**

- Axiom 8: **Movement in one direction of a structural conflict will precipitate compensating movement in the other direction.**

- Axiom 9: **Structure seeks equilibrium.**

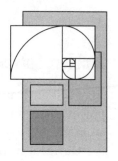

CHAPTER 4

The Problem with Problem Solving

Before we explore the most prevalent structural conflicts that organizations face, as we will do in Chapter 5, we must take a look at problem solving, because a problem-solving mindset leads to a common misperception of the structural forces that cause the organization to behave as it does. Were we to study structural conflicts as problems to solve, we would not understand them as *structural* phenomena. We would look for solutions rather than understanding. We would ask, How do we get rid of them? rather than, What is causing our organization to oscillate? In order to redesign an organization so that it can advance, we need to discern the actual forces in play, rather than simply address unwanted symptoms.

Too often, problem solving is used by managers as the primary approach in mobilizing their people. This is unfortunate, because problem solving is an inadequate approach for building an organization and growing a business. Problem solving has a built-in structural tendency to oscillate. Let's examine the structure.

Problem Solving and Oscillation

In traditional problem-solving techniques, we start our thought process by defining a problem. Then the unwanted problematic situation provokes actions designed to eliminate the difficulty.

Our goal in this process is to get rid of the problem. The more intense the problem seems to be, the more incentive there is to rid ourselves of it. But by taking action, we reduce the intensity of the problem. We feel better about the situation because we feel we are addressing it. And, while the problem may not yet be solved, there often is a degree of improvement in the situation that reduces the problem's intensity. However, once the problem is less intense, there is less incentive to act.

Here's how the structure cycles through, forming an oscillating pattern:

1. High intensity of the problem

Problem

2. Leads to action taken to solve it

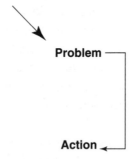

3. Leads to *less* intensity of the problem

4. Leads to *less* action

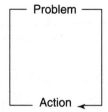

5. Leads to the problem's re-intensifying if unsolved

This structure leads to a predictable pattern of oscillation. More intensity leads to more action, which reduces some of the intensity of the problem, which leads to less action. At best, this strategy can work short-term to eradicate what we don't want. It cannot help us create what we do want.

In organizations that center their management style on problem solving,[1] different problems shift into dominance over time. With each new squeaky wheel, other squeaky wheels lose their fascination and importance. If action has been taken to rid the company of a particular problem, the intensity of that problem may be significantly reduced; even if the problem itself doesn't change, or gets worse, other problems will become more important and influential.

A problem-solving organization cannot advance. If problem solving is the major organizing principle within a company, it cannot be structured to advance, and therefore it will oscillate, for the following reasons:

1. Actions will not be taken to move us toward our aspirations.

---

[1] *Problem solving* is the most commonly used term within organizations. Another use of the term is found in mathematics and engineering, in which problem solving is not motivated by eliminating an undesirable condition, but by bringing forth desired information, such as the sum of a column of numbers.

Instead, they will be a reaction to the problems. People will be motivated by what they do *not* want, rather than what they *do* want.

2. There is a difference between building demolition and architecture.

One is taking action to have something go away, the other is taking action to have something come into being. This is the difference between problem solving and driving the organization by a vision of what we want to accomplish.

3. Organizational learning is limited to how to eliminate unwanted situations, not how to bring about desired situations.

Therefore, learning would not provide the organization with added competency and capacity. And, if the problem-solving tactic is truly successful, the problem will go away, leaving little application for learning in the future.

4. Motivation for action shifts from one problem to another as problems change in importance over time.

5. A false impression of effectiveness is created within the organization, leading to questionable values (for example, that the time to act is when there is a crisis).

During the heyday of problem-based management styles in the seventies and early eighties, many companies discovered that some of the best firefighters within their organizations also turned out to be the pyromaniacs! The more rewards that were given for dealing with crises, the greater was the number of calamities. Some companies found that when they got rid of the firefighters many of the fires went out.

6. Problems dictate a biased viewpoint.

Problem solving tends to bias our viewpoint and prejudice our choice of process. For example, if we defined the problem as lack of capital, the solution would be get more capital. But if we defined the problem as poor management systems, we would attempt to change them. If we said that the problem was that people are not taking personal responsibility for their work, we might try to empower them. If we said that our products did not have enough quality built-in to them, we would begin to try to build in quality.

These descriptions of reality might be accurate on the level of symptoms. But these symptoms are described out of context of causes, and "solutions" do not lead to lasting change. Problem solving can drive a flurry of actions that merely shift various symptoms around, and it is not always obvious how poorly it has worked to get an organization where it wants to be.

These days, many managers begin almost every conversation with the phrase "The problem is . . . " This focuses people on problems and their solutions. By using this form, people begin to arrange their activities around a search-and-destroy mission against problems. Too often this way of thinking gives people the impression that they are doing something important, but in actuality they are usually filling their time correcting the effects created by faulty structural design. Chronic problem solving as a management tool leads to mindlessness and lack of critical thought, because when we organize our process around problems we do not have to think at all. In a sense, our problems do our thinking for us; the problems we confront tell us what to do.

Clearly chronic problem solving within an organization demonstrates a lack of essential planning and organizational control. Of course, organizations do have problems and do need to deal with them well. But the better designed the business is, the less likely it will be that problem solving is its primary orientation.

TQM, Problem Solving, and Structure

Some people adopt a system like TQM as if it were a problem-solving process. Let's look at the structure of continuous improvement when used that way. We begin with the current condition, analyze it, and then improve it.

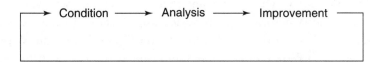

Condition ⟶ Analysis ⟶ Improvement

The driving, or generative force within this process is found within the current condition. The analysis is designed to find imperfections within the current conditions. Improvements are designed to eliminate imperfections. Over time, fewer and fewer imperfections will be found as the improvements work. However, the process is moving toward *inertia* as the driving force or generative energy reduces over time. Ironically, in this structure, *more* quality leads to *less* action toward improvements over time.

One of the best aspects of some total quality approaches is that an entire system of relationships is considered, rather than simply local events. However, often people attempting to use TQM lose their system-wide focus as they begin to work with incremental process improvements.

Redesigning the Oscillating Structure

In the condition-analysis-adjustment cycle, we can redesign the structure by establishing structural tension.

First, we locate our desired end result. What do we want to create? This question needs to be considered from a broader perspective than simply "the best quality possible" or "customer satisfaction." In fact, when incremental improvement is adopted within an entire TQM approach, it must be tied to the organization's overall business strategy; then goals such as "minimal production variation tied to customer loyalty" can be the starting point for determining the desired state. If these goals are developed in a vacuum, however, they become meaningless in the broader picture.

So-called zero defects, motivated by problems within a current production approach, do not lead to new processes that are more efficient, cost effective, or innovative, because they do not help us define the desired end results our actions should support. With an understanding of our actual goals, *process redesign may lead to an invention of entirely new processes that make the current ones, no matter how beautifully perfected, obsolete.*

Once we know what results any process we choose serves, we can begin to build structural tension by defining a vision of what we want to create, and our current reality in relationship to that vision. Within that structural frame, our quality-improvement process will become transformed from one that produces inertia to one that produces momentum. Continual improvement can become part of the action plan that moves us from our current state to our desired state, as shown in the illustration.

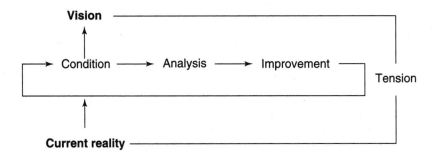

Those organizations that succeed brilliantly at a total quality approach are framed within structural tension, and systematic improvements do not happen in a vacuum. The desired outcomes are clear to everyone who is working on the improvement of processes. Current reality is gauged by accurate statistical measurements and other instruments of observation and analysis. The desired state—our vision—is brought into being, helped by the improvement in the process. Relevant standards can be defined to measure that improvement: Where are we in relationship to our vision?

Unfortunately, many organizations who have used a total quality approach, reengineering, or other fundamental change systems do so from a problem-solving frame of reference, and thus the real advantages of such approaches are barely realized, because the underlying structure leads to oscillation, not to advancement.

United States Air Force Lt. Colonel Larry Willers, of Wright Laboratory, has used both TQM and the structural approach in his work as an in-house trainer and structural consultant. Here is what he had to say:

> As an Air Force laboratory, we knew we needed to continually improve in order to maintain our viability as an organization. We saw Total Quality Management as the way to do it. And we did improve our employee's awareness, interpersonal skills, and understanding of customer focus and process. But we were unable to fundamentally improve the way we conduct business. Our people care about their work and do want to do it better. But they were frustrated that their efforts had made little difference. The reason was that we had made no fundamental change to the structure of our organization.

Once we understood the structural forces in play, we were able to design a structure which clearly moves us toward our goals. We are now focused on our customers' needs and targeting our technology research and TQM efforts within the frame of structural tension. And, we were able to change the structure without disturbing the basic organizational leadership hierarchy. People are in the same positions, reporting to the exact same people, but how they make decisions has been fundamentally altered to support our goals, rather than simply solve problems. It is great to realize you can make real progress.

As we explore the structural approach, it is important to remember that structural dynamics is not a problem-solving technique but a study of structure that requires an understanding of how structure works and how to redesign our organizations so that the underlying structure supports our aspirations.

Quick Review

- Problem solving is a common approach toward management, but it creates an oscillating pattern of behavior because, as problems are solved, the motivation for action is reduced.

- This oscillation is reflected in the organization's behavior: Actions are initiated in reaction to problems, not to achieve desired results; actions focus on eliminating problems, not on bringing something into existence; organizational learning is limited to problems and diminishes as the problems diminish; the organization's focus changes from one problem to another, even if the initial problem remains; causes (the ultimate problems) can become the organization's primary focus; and problems dictate our actions.

- At best, problem solving rids the company of what it doesn't want. It does not produce what is wanted.

- When TQM or other change systems are used as problem-solving devices, they do not work. This is because the generative force within the condition-analysis-improvement cycle moves toward oscillation as improvements are made. However, when this cycle is placed into the context of structural tension, it moves toward advancement.

CHAPTER 5

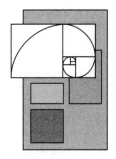

Organizational Structural Conflicts

Chapter 3 used change versus continuity to illustrate the form structural conflicts take. In this chapter, we are going to describe some of the other major structural conflicts that managers must contend with throughout their organizational lives. By examining common structural conflicts, not only can we gain insight into these specific areas, but we will also be better able to identify *other* structural conflicts that may exist in the organization.

It is an inescapable law of structure that structural conflicts produce an oscillating pattern of behavior (the third law of organizational structure). So when organizations oscillate, we will be able to find various structural conflicts that are dominant. We begin by examining a structural conflict that limits growth and sends the organization into an oscillating pattern that moves between growth and limitation.

Growth and Limitation

Organizations are in the business of expanding their operation in many areas—markets, profits, product mix, customer service, scale, and scope, for example. Most managers rightfully see the general growth of the company as one of their major responsibilities. So why do many organizations experience critical limitations when they attempt to grow the company? The answer lies in a structural conflict between growth and capacity.

The desire to expand is resolved by growing the company.

But as we grow, we stress the organization's capacity. Growth increases the workload, which will lead to:

- The same number of people doing more work, or

- New people being added

If the same number of people are doing significantly more work, they become less effective. Management may hope to reorganize the way people work so that greater productivity will come from the same number of people. Usually this idea looks good on paper but fails in reality. An increased workload does not often lead to new and inventive procedures for two reasons. First, the worst time to ask people to adopt new methods is when they are feeling overwhelmed. Second, there is a learning curve associated with adopting new methods: people are almost always *less* efficient before they learn to be *more* efficient. Faced with increasing demands, they tend to lapse into familiar, "tried and true" work habits rather than taking on new and unfamiliar methods.

If we add more people to do extra work, the workload will not decrease at once because the new people need to be trained. Who will train them? The very people whose workload has just increased. New people will *add* to the strain on capacity before they are able to reduce the workload.

A similar phenomenon occurs when new technology is added to increase productivity of the existing work force. The learning curve needed to master the new systems strains capacity temporarily before it is of any real help.

Measures designed to increase capacity come up against the current level of capacity, which can seem fixed. This produces a strain on capacity, leading to a shift in dominance to a second tension-resolution system. The tension driving this second tension-resolution system is the discrepancy between *actual capacity* of the organization and the *amount of capacity demanded* by growth that has taken place.

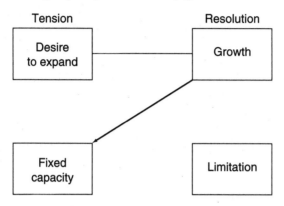

The more growth there is, the more that capacity is strained. Fixed capacity becomes the dominant system, and resolves itself by limiting growth.

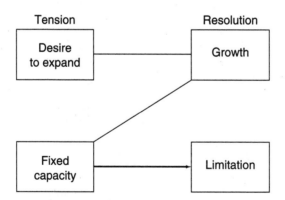

Once growth is limited, strain on capacity decreases and everyone breathes a little easier for a while. But once the relationship between capacity and limitation become less discrepant, the desire to grow becomes the dominant theme once again.

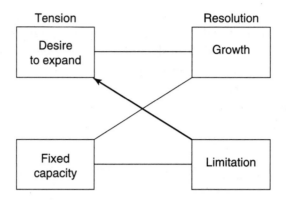

This is a common pattern in organizations:

- People start out on a course aimed at growth
- As volume of the company's activities increase, capacity becomes strained
- Growth slows down as people shift their attention to managing capacity issues

Usually capacity is not fixed, but it takes a longer time to increase capacity than to produce growth. The lag time functions as if capacity were fixed, or at least fixed at a rate that is too slow for the desired rate of expansion. Thus the high growth in, say, sales, conflicts with the limited expansion rate of capacity, say, manufacturing.

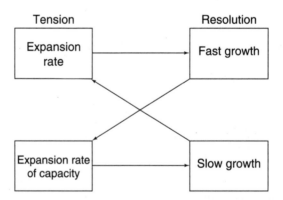

The relationship between capacity and growth is a vital element in the overall success of the organization's expansion goals. Unfortunately, management of this vital relationship often is haphazardly conceived. Many companies neglect important questions of capacity through an informal generalized policy of minimizing the cost of doing business. In some organizations, workloads are strained to a point that only work-aholics can survive in the stress-filled environment. Everyone is so busy they do not have time to reflect on the *way* they work, therefore they are unlikely to invent more efficient and effective methods. They may want to change, and even hire consultants who offer useful advice, but they're unable to take the advice because they're just too busy. "This is our culture," people proclaim almost proudly, as if there were something destined about their chronic overload. In these organizations, the last thing people want is more work, so attempts to grow and expand are met with great resistance and the organization begins to oscillate.

Types of Conflict

The Workload–Budget Conflict

In some organizations, senior management delivers conflicting messages: "Meet your growth goals and minimize your expenses." In the following structural conflict chart, we see a shift of dominance from themes of strained workload to those of budgetary concerns, resulting in expansion, then downsizing only a few years later. A few years after that, more people are added once again to meet the pressures of an understaffed organization.

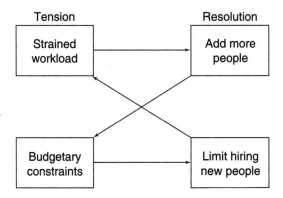

Adding more people conflicts with budgetary constraints, and limiting new people conflicts with the strained workload. The organization oscillates.

The Profit–Capacity Conflict

Another, related structural conflict makes a comprehensive strategy of balancing growth and capacity unlikely. It occurs when profit goals are in contention with the desire to expand capacity. The debate often occurs between financial people, who are trained to think in terms of limiting costs, and the managers, who think in terms of accomplishing the work of the company (see the illustration at the top of the next page).

The increased cost from expanding capacity conflicts with profit goals, and limiting costs to improve profits conflicts with the desire to expand capacity.

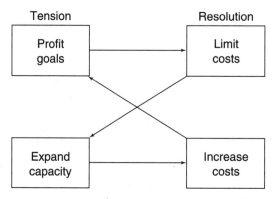

From a business perspective, investing in increased capacity is included in the cost of doing business; it is a requirement. But to financially oriented managers, this cost is a needless expense. In a structural conflict, these two points of view are more than a philosophical disagreement. The structural conflict leads to oscillations between times when pressure is on to turn in a good financial performance and times when expanding capacity is deemed necessary to stay competitive in the marketplace. As oscillation occurs, one, and then the other, point of view becomes the basis for determining policy and strategy.

Similar to the conflict between profit and expanded capacity is the conflict between profit and an expanding business. This produces an oscillating pattern of interrupted business expansion and inconsistent profit configurations as major corporate decisions shift from a business focus to a financial focus, pitting managers against stockholders, and long-term interests against short-term ones.

The Business–Profit Conflict

Investing to expand the business conflicts with cutting costs to expand profits.

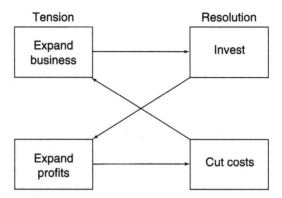

Wall Street has a lot to answer for when it comes to the economic fate many corporations have suffered in recent years. In the past, people who invested in stocks usually tried to pick well-respected companies, then held the stock for many years, perhaps even passing it along to their children. Holding stock helped the company invest in its long-term future. Investment in stock was supportive of long-range benefits for both company and stockholder. But that type of thinking has radically changed in recent times.

Nowadays, those who invest in stock achieve their major return on investment when the stock is sold—not held. Stockbrokers make money by trading stocks, so they are interested in more transactions—not fewer ones. This makes the short-term performance of stock more important to the investors than the long-term viability of the company. A gambler's fever now afflicts many investors. This has led to a devastating structural conflict that forces those in senior management positions to make decisions that are not in the best interests of the company. Here's how it works.

What do investors in stock want? High return on investment.

What does the organization want? Capital to invest in development of the enterprise. But when capital is used for reinvestment, immediate return on investment often goes down, and money available for shareholders' dividends is reduced until the investment can be recouped by growth.

A conflict of interest develops between the shareholders and the organization, producing oscillation:

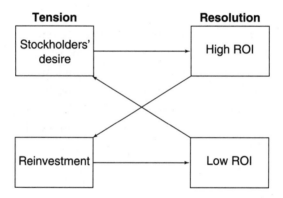

At first the focus within the organization is growing the business. New plants are built or new technology developed, costing money and time. But no one knows for sure if these additions will increase the company's fortunes, and, as the investment is implemented, performance of the stock begins to fall; the immediate attractiveness of the stock declines based on the company's unpredictable future.

Stock performance affects the organization's cost of capital; money becomes more expensive. Other companies whose stock is performing better in the market can borrow money at lower interest rates and enjoy a competitive advantage. The company begins to look vulnerable, and images of hostile take-overs loom on the horizon. A crisis develops, and senior management is asked to focus on the performance of the stock. The organization reconsiders its position, and begins to work toward making its stock more attractive to the stock market. The focus shifts from reinvestment to profit and high performance of the stock—from business development to financial management. Then, once the stock is performing well and the company's competitors threaten, it reverts to a focus on long-term reinvestment strategies.

This structural conflict will produce shifts in managerial focus over several years, and lead the organization to instability oscillation between short- and long-term strategies.

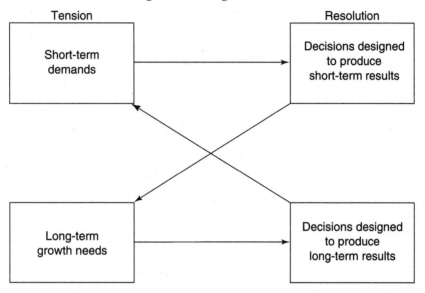

Let's look at this structural phenomenon from the perspective of our rubber-band analogy. As we move toward our long-term goals, short-term demands increase tension on the opposing rubber band. Where is it easier for us to go? In the direction of addressing short-term demands that require our immediate attention.

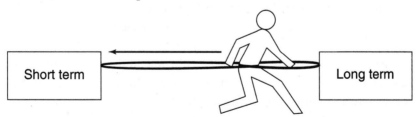

We begin to address the issues that call for our immediate attention. But as we do, the need to concentrate on our longer-term strategies once again demands consideration. Now, where is it easier for us to go? Back to questions of long-term strategy.

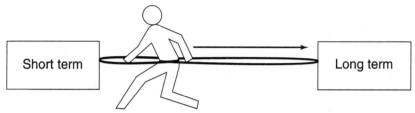

This structural conflict produces fluctuation in leadership and direction. It seems as if the organization can't make up its mind. Does it want to develop its long-range plans of reinvesting in the company, or is it in the business of selling stock? Senior management's oscillating behavior between these two points can lead to appalling decisions that undermine morale and organizational alignment.

Many Western corporations have fallen victim to this structure as companies have merged, been acquired, changed management, changed direction, and even changed industries.

This structure is less dominant in Asia, particularly in the great Japanese companies. Why? Because long-term planning produces structural tension as the organizing principle, and conflicts of interests are managed within that frame. The entire organization is governed with its eye on its desirable end results. Changes are monitored carefully and tactics adjusted accordingly.

For many organizations in the West, long-term planning seems like a luxury. Often the plans they make are less about organizing the business and more about propaganda for banks, annual reports, and public relations. Usually these plans do not take into consideration structural conflicts driving the organization away from where it wants to be. Hardly anyone thinks about changing the structure, because management is caught up in a reactive / responsive pattern of oscillation which is driven by a long-term / short-term structural conflict.

True long-term planning, capable of focusing the organization on well-conceived end results, will be restricted as long as this type of structural conflict is in play. CEOs will come and go, but unless they can change the organization's underlying structure from a dominance of structural conflicts to structural tension, none of them—no matter what their management style or temperament—will be able to create more than minor shifts of oscillation.

We hear a lot about new management style these days. Cross-functional teams are said to break down the walls of miscommunication and encourage people to think more systemically. Decision making is being pushed down further into the organization, becoming decentralized, transforming what was autocratic management into management of a consensual type. What was once proprietary information is now distributed throughout the organization. As stock options are made available to members of the organization, they are encouraged to think of themselves as owners. Managers are also encouraged to treat their people with dignity and respect, and the employee's health and general well-being are promoted as a high value that will lead to company loyalty. All of these trends sound enlightened, indeed. Yet, when many organizations attempt to implement these practices, the byproduct is often confusion and instability.

A common complaint of senior management is that people hesitate to make decisions once they have been given the authority to do so. Another is that, although cross-functional teams have productive work sessions, their actual plans tend to be put on hold. Though members are encouraged to think from a wider organizational perspective, they still think and act out of local concerns. With all the talk about how people should be treated and how they should act, political intrigues still dominate the scene. Why are these good ideas about management not always as useful as they should be? The answer is found in various structural conflicts that determine an organization's behavioral tendencies.

The Decentralization–Centralization Conflict

In the past, organizations had excessive layers of management that served to centralize control. Decisions were made by people who were not always close to those the decisions affected. This unwieldy situation burdened many organizations with slow response times and unrealistic plans.

To many, it began to make sense that those who are affected by decisions should be involved with the decision-making process. Their judgment should be the soundest and, since they will have been involved in making the decision, their implementation should be more effective. It was hoped that more people making decisions in strategic locales would lead to more managerial capacity, so in recent years many organizations attempted to decentralize their decision-making process.

This change was more radical than it might seem at first glance.

Decisions are a medium of *power*. By pushing decisions down into the organization, power is being distributed more widely. More power everywhere means less power concentrated in the hands of a few. Those who succeeded in their careers as managers did so because they knew how to make decisions. They kept a large degree of control in their own hands, assuring themselves that things were being done properly. Most managers see themselves as responsible for maintaining control of the work processes to assure the group's success.

When decision making was decentralized, successful managers were asked to relinquish some of their control. Many of them found this hard to do. A manager's desire to control outcomes leads him or her to make all major decisions, which then are implemented by other people in the organization. Here is the structural conflict faced by the managers and those they managed.

But the manager may lack vital information that people closer to the situation confront daily. This leads to a desire to have those people able to make decisions so that they can address immediate concerns in a timely way.

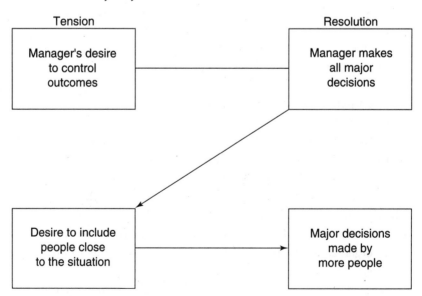

But when more decisions are made by more people, the manager has less control over outcomes. This situation feels unstable to many managers. Tension on the manager builds. Soon, the manager's desire to control the outcome becomes dominant again, and he or she reclaims the power to make all major decisions.

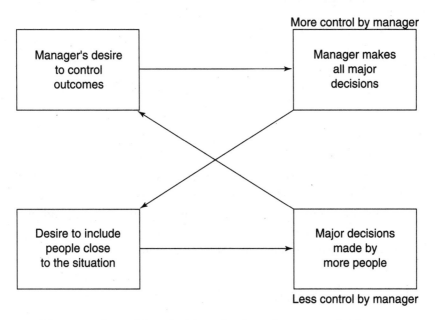

More people making decisions leads to less control. Fewer people making decisions leads to more control. The result is an oscillation between centralized and decentralized decision making.

And what of the people who are given new power to decide? We would expect them to seize the opportunity of playing a bigger role in their organization. Surprisingly, they often do not. Many people are uncomfortable with their new power and avoid making decisions. Why?

When we are given decision-making power, we also are given a degree of accountability. We may fail. Most organizations do not know how to deal with failure judiciously. Failure is usually an unforgivable mistake that leads to punishment of one sort or another. When that's the case, everyone avoids making mistakes.

Decentralized decision making goes hand in hand with widely distributed accountability. Because the potential threat of failure goes up proportionally with the degree of power, people are *less* likely than ever before to make decisions.

Here is a structural look at the phenomenon:

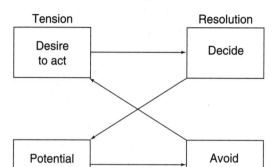

People want to act so they can participate in the enterprise. But, when they begin to make decisions, the risk factor increases. They resolve the risk by avoiding decisions that are potentially hazardous. From the structure, we begin to understand why people seem to be behaving in inconsistent ways. Forces in play are changing and people are acting accordingly. They are, in fact, responding quite naturally to a built-in conflict within the organization.

The Growth–Stability Conflict

Decentralized decision making is designed to support growth within an organization because, when there are more people who are able to decide, an organization's management capacity is increased. Instead, it often leads to oscillations between growth and instability.

An elegant structural description of this behavior is found in a structural conflict between growth and stability, which can lead an organization to a pattern of oscillating behavior.

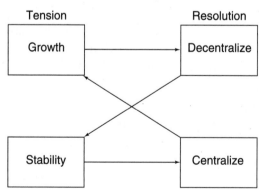

In this structural conflict, desire for growth leads to decentralization of decision making. However, even if growth occurs, decentralization creates instability. Once there is a shift of dominance, stability becomes more desired than growth and decisions are centralized again.

Layers of Structural Conflicts

Usually several structural conflicts are occurring simultaneously within a single organization. The *growth-stability* conflict often coexists with the *change-continuity* conflict. The *invest-cut costs* conflict, the *decentralized-centralized decision making, autocratic-consensual management styles,* and the *short-term–long-term* conflicts add overlapping layers of structural conflicts.

Patterns of oscillation may take several years to repeat and may move so slowly that it is difficult to pinpoint just what is causing the changes, but the inexorable pull of the structure is felt by everyone.

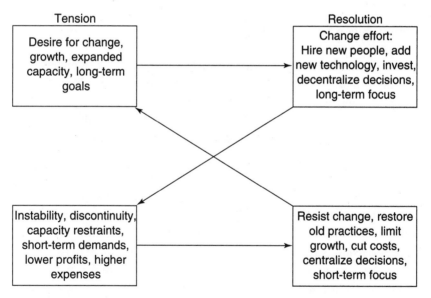

When several structural conflicts are in operation simultaneously, there is often an experience of desperate struggle as people fight against something that seems beyond their control. Moreover, another more-subtle impact penetrates the organization—resignation and hopelessness. There is a feeling that nothing works and that fate, more than imagination and diligence, will decide the company's future.

Changes in leadership may temporarily suspend collective experience of fatalism, but if the structure remains unchanged, the honeymoon with any new leadership is soon over and people return to a profound sense of powerlessness. Only this time it is even worse than before, because a glimmer of hope has proven to be merely an illusion.

Management may try to shake the organization out of this malaise with positive motivational furor: "C'mon, everyone! We can do it! We only need to believe in ourselves!"

Or, it may try a "slap in the face" approach with warnings about possible negative consequences. This is done in the hope that the organization will come to its senses and say "Thanks! I needed that."

Temporary benefits may result from either method, but neither will succeed long term. Carrots and sticks cannot change inadequate structures. We must begin to think in terms of redesigning the company's structure so that change will lead beyond chronic patterns of oscillation and move to structural advancement.

Identifying Structural Conflicts

While the various structural conflicts explored in this chapter are found in many organizations, we can better understand the structural forces in play when we can recognize them in our own organizations. One way to explore this is by identifying patterns of oscillating behaviors that exist within your organization. The time frame may be months, or even a few years. Choose a typical one. What is the first swing in the oscillating pattern? As the organization begins to move in that direction, what is the shift away from that swing? Once you have chosen such a pattern to use as part of this exercise, look at tension-resolution systems that drive each side of the oscillation. Remember: a tension is formed by the discrepancy or difference between two elements—often a desired state in contrast to a current state. As that tension-resolution system moves toward resolution, notice how it exacerbates the tension in the competing system. This will help you understand the nature of the behavior you have observed. You can note the structural conflict by filling in this form: .

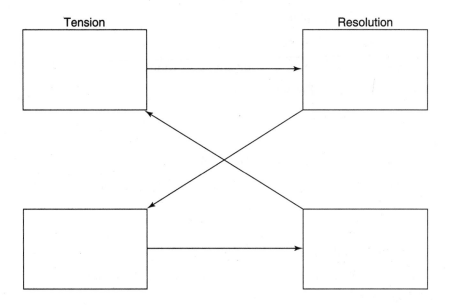

Once people understand the structural conflicts that drive an oscillating pattern, they can begin a dialogue with colleagues in which everyone can begin to explore built-in organizational structural dynamics. This process is tremendously useful because it affords everyone a greater perspective by which to view reality in an objective way.

While structural conflicts fill the organizational landscape, we are not stuck with them. The next chapter introduces the key principle that enables us to redesign organizations so as to eliminate structural conflicts.

Quick Review

- Organizations oscillate because of structural conflicts, and insights can be gained by examining some of the more common ones.

- Organizations oscillate between:
  - Expansion and limitation
  - Strained workload and budgetary constraints
  - Profit goals and expansion goals
  - Investment and cost cutting
  - Stock performance and reinvestment
  - Short-term and long-term demands
  - Desire to control and desire to include others in decision making
  - Desire to act and potential risk
  - Growth and stability
- Layers of structural conflicts combine to create a wider magnitude of oscillation.
- By observing examples of oscillation in your own organization, you can begin to describe the competing tension-resolution systems that form the structural conflict. This will enable you to better understand the structural forces in play and to begin a useful dialogue with colleagues.

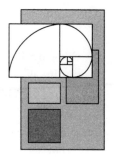

CHAPTER 6

The Principle of Hierarchy
The Key to Structural Redesign

Structural conflicts are not problems to be solved, but structures that need to be redesigned. This chapter introduces the key principle in redesigning structural conflicts—that of *hierarchy*.

The Desired Outcome

Let's revisit the change-continuity structural conflict to show the first step toward building structural tension when a structural conflict exists. Here is the structural conflict:

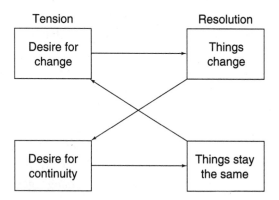

73

A desire for change leads to change, which begets a desire for continuity, which leads to avoidance of change. But once continuity has been reestablished, the desire for change reemerges.

In order to move from structural conflict to structural tension, we first need to identify what we really want: *What is our desired outcome?*

What *do* we really want? In this case, we want two outcomes, both change and continuity. But to the degree that we change the organization continuity is lost, and to the degree that we hold on to continuity change is resisted. How do we address this dilemma?

Hierarchy of Importance

While both goals may be important to us, one will be more important than the other:

- **Change** may be more important than continuity

- **Continuity** may be more important than change

Consequently, we must create a hierarchy of importance. First, we determine our primary goal—the one that is more important than any competing goal. Once we have done that, we can organize a new structure which has structural tension.

In the change-continuity example, change itself is a process conceived to serve some particular result or desired outcome—one that would be accomplished once change has been successfully completed. Before creating a hierarchy, we must be clear about the desired outcomes that the change is attempting to produce. Why do we want to change? To improve our products? Our management systems? Our relationship with suppliers? To grow our market share? develop customer loyalty? Or, to better our efficiency and effectiveness? Once we have answered these questions, we can form a change goal.

Then we need to evaluate our current level of continuity. Organizations are in the habit of constructing strategies for change without considering the degree of continuity they want to maintain while the change effort is being implemented. How much continuity do we need to maintain? How much discontinuity can we live with? Once we answer these questions, we can form a continuity goal.

Since the desire for change leads to a departure from the norm, our continuity goal will be formed by our change goal—the more change, the less continuity. However, we may find that our change goal is impossible to achieve in the short run because the resulting discontinuity may work against us. This situation provides us with an opportunity to rethink our desires.

Which is more important to us:

- Fast change that may be disruptive to the organization?, or

- Longer-term implementation of change that will help us maintain a consistent level of continuity?

If we need to accomplish change in a strategic time frame because it is crucial to our success, we might choose to pursue our change goal, knowing full well that continuity will be undermined. Of course, we would not want a prolonged period of discontinuity, but we might decide to permit the situation to exist temporarily. In this case, the change goal is senior to the continuity goal.

If our change goal does not need to be accomplished immediately, we might decide to build a firm base of organizational continuity, paving the way for the transition before we attempt drastic change. In this case, our continuity goal will be senior to our change goal, and we will regulate change by continuity. The more continuity, the less change; the less continuity, the more change.

Let's illustrate the hierarchy of importance with a case study. In order to increase their sales volume, the sales and marketing departments of a large pharmaceutical company formulated a plan to change their marketing approach radically. Instead of a single nationwide strategy with each product line marketed to doctors by a different sales force, they proposed to use fewer sales people selling a greater variety of products, and to develop local marketing strategies tailored to each geographical area. Their idea was based on two major considerations: (1) that each area of the country had a unique consumer mix (Florida, for example, has a larger elderly population than most other parts of the country), and (2) that doctors do not like to be besieged by salespeople.

The sales and marketing departments were enthusiastic about their ideas, and held a meeting with senior management to propose the plan. Senior management rejected it almost immediately—not because the idea was poorly conceived, but because they were unwilling to adopt an unknown and untested marking strategy over one that was generating the company's major revenue source. The change might have worked brilliantly, but management did not want to put the economic continuity of the business in jeopardy.[1] Their interest in continuity was greater than their interest in change, even though the change was designed to increase sales volume. Change in the marketing strategy would need to be organized in the context of economic continuity and utilize such things as pilot programs in selected regions or single experiments to study the efficacy of the strategy.

Either change or continuity can predominate, but they cannot be equal. Therefore it is necessary to determine which is the more important value. Once we do that, we have created a hierarchy. We have determined our primary goal. *Our primary goal will be the focal point in organizing structural tension, and the other goal or goals will be designed to support it.*

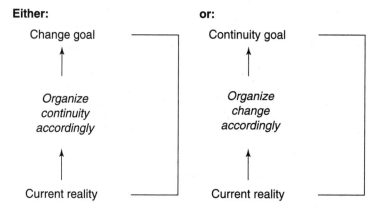

Either:

Change goal

↑

*Organize
continuity
accordingly*

↑

Current reality

or:

Continuity goal

↑

*Organize
change
accordingly*

↑

Current reality

When we move from structural conflict to structural tension, we are defining our more important objective, our primary goal. The goal in the competing tension-resolution system is then reorganized to be supportive of the primary goal, rather than conflicting with it. If change is our more important goal, we will be prepared to manage the resulting discontinuity that may occur to support our change effort. If continuity is our more important goal, we will manage any

---

[1]Many organizations have damaged their economic base by managing change haphazardly. The relationship with customers can suffer when products are changed or services are disrupted. There are many examples. The most famous example of this disruptive change is when Coke changed its formula, and consumers were outraged. When Jaguar changed the classic curvaceous lines of its XJ6 sedan and gave it a boxy, nondescript design, customers felt betrayed.

change efforts to minimize significant disruption. Once we know our primary desired outcomes, we are able to organize competing outcomes accordingly.

The Drive for Equilibrium

One technical way to describe the change from a structure that contains two competing tension-resolution systems to one that contains only one dominant tension-resolution system is to study each structure from the standpoint of equilibrium. Remember Axiom 9 tells us that structure seeks equilibrium. Equilibrium is the point of balance—the midpoint—between two competing goals. This is an important insight, because once we understand that structure has its own goal, independent from ours, we can attempt to align our goal with that of the structure.

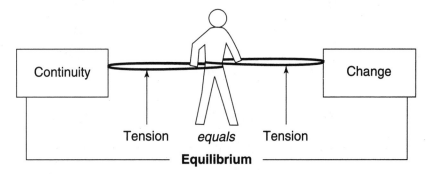

This technical point helps us to understand the true mechanism in force when there is either a structural conflict or a structural tension in play. We can understand structure as a force in nature, rather than simply a metaphor or a problem to be solved. This next structural axiom sheds light on the state of equilibrium when a goal is reached in each type of structure.

AXIOM 10

- In an oscillating structure, the fulfillment of a desire produces a high state of non-equilibrium.

- In a resolving structure, the fulfillment of a desire produces a state of equilibrium.

If we think in terms of states of equilibrium, we can see that the same event—that of reaching a goal—has a completely different dynamic in an oscillating from that of an advancing or resolving structure. Success, in an organization that oscillates, creates a state of most non-equilibrium. The structure's response to the state of non-equilibrium is to move away from the success in order to restore equilibrium. This is why "success cannot succeed in an organization that oscillates" is an inescapable law of organizational structure.

On the other hand, when structural tension is the dominant structure, there is only one primary goal—the desired state—and a state of non-equilibrium exists when the current reality differs from that desired state (when the goal has yet to be reached). Success brings a state of equilibrium, because the goal has been achieved; therefore, all the tension driving the action has been resolved. New creations, goals, strategies, and technology may be desired in the future, and the new desires create a new state of non-equilibrium when compared to their current reality. But, within structural tension, the state of non-equilibrium can lead to a state of equilibrium as soon as the current state matches the desired state.

From Structural Conflict to Structural Tension

When we discover structural conflicts, we can design a structure that is capable of full resolution. When we establish a hierarchy between the two competing tensions, we are able to form a structure that can resolve. Therefore, success can succeed. Rather than leading to a structural inevitability that must move away from a state of non-equilibrium, it becomes a state of equilibrium that can be built upon.

Let us illustrate this using the growth-stability structural conflict.

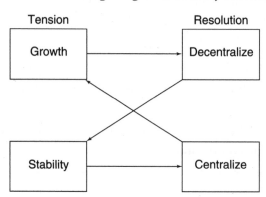

In this case, decentralized decision making intended to promote growth conflicts with stability, and the centralized decision making intended to achieve stability conflicts with growth.

Once we determine which is more important to us, stability or growth, this structural conflict can be converted into structural tension. Then we can redesign the structure by establishing goals that reflect our hierarchy of values, and support it managerially.

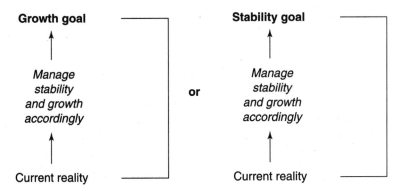

Most structural conflicts in organizations can be addressed by establishing hierarchies. But establishing hierarchies is not all there is to the process of structural redesign. We must also put into place new structures that support our aims, our aspirations, our ambitions, and our purpose.

The next few chapters will discuss how to identify the organizational purpose and create business and management strategies using structural tension.

Quick Review

- Establishing a hierarchy between competing goals is the key to structural redesign.

- When we move from structural conflict to structural tension, we are defining our primary goal. This action reorganizes the relationship between competing goals.

- This is a change from a structure that contains two competing tension-resolution systems to a structure that contains only one dominant tension-resolution system.

- Axiom 10: **In an oscillating structure, the fulfillment of a desire produces a high state of non-equilibrium. In a resolving structure, the fulfillment of a desire produces a state of equilibrium.**

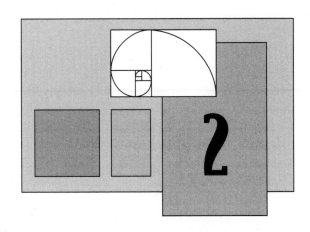

Elements
of
Design

From Organizational
Oscillation to Advancement

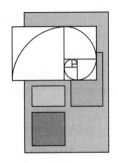

CHAPTER 7

Self-Organizing Systems and the Principle of Thematic Unity

The Thematic Unifying Principle

The great value of an organization is that people can join together and, by their concerted effort, accomplish feats that would be impossible for any individual to achieve alone. The organization is not an organic phenomenon of nature. It is a refined human invention that requires the coordination of countless activities. What ties these activities together? Usually a common cause or purpose.

Most organizations have a unique purpose. Usually people are not able to articulate the purpose entirely, at least not in words. This is not because the purpose is intangible but because much of it is simply *beyond* words. A great deal of its profundity exists on a nonverbal level. Nonetheless people can feel it, and generally they agree with it. That is why they experience genuine frustration when the organization acts in ways that are inconsistent with what could be called its "spiritual" purpose.

An organization can have an authentic sense of purpose and yet fail to use this strength as its prime thematic organizing principle. The purpose is made irrelevant, but it does not go away. Instead, it goes underground, waiting to be expressed.

An organization that *does* understand its direction and purpose is a different matter entirely. All decisions can be measured against them: Are decisions consistent with the purpose and direction? From disciplining the organization's strategies and policies to aligning actions they take, to learning what needs to be learned, to fusing direction with aspiration, you can be sure that a thematic unifying principle is alive and well within the organization.

Paradoxically, just as organizations by nature have a common purpose, their typical division of labor can work against this purpose. Organizations have the advantage and disadvantage of being divided into sections. The advantage: Not everyone has to duplicate the same efforts. The disadvantage: Each section does not always know how to coordinate activities with the other sections, particularly if they have not articulated a comprehensive principle to link diverse activities.

One of the major points of this book is this: *An organization can be structured to advance and succeed. But it takes more than good intentions, vision, open and honest conversation, and enlightened attitudes. It takes good structural design work that ties the parts together thematically.*

In the arts, this factor is called the thematic unifying principle. All great masterpieces exhibit strong thematic unifying principles that govern their structural designs.

Too often organizations fail to build such a unifying device into their designs. A question that often reveals the lack of such an organizing principle is this: "How do you folks make decisions around here?" Often, the question is answered by strange looks, accompanied by hems and haws, until some incomprehensible explanation is attempted. Other times some people simply say, "That's a good question." A tell-tale sign of a weak or missing unifying principle is an inconsistent decision-making process.

The Bankruptcy of the Vision, Purpose, and Mission Statement

Many organizations attempt to have a thematic unifying principle by constructing a purpose statement, a mission statement, or a vision statement. With a plaque on the office wall, they try to convince themselves that they have defined their unifying intentions. But no one is fooled by the rhetoric. Such statements are rarely seen as *the* guiding force that determines the major decisions.

The instinct to create mission statements is correct: it stems from the desire to tie the organization together by constructing an overriding theme. But the manifestation of the instinct misses the mark. It is astonishing how many organizations have mission statements that are ignored by almost everyone. It is even more astonishing how senior managers fail to recognize the lack of influence these statements have on the organization. The emperor has no clothes, but many pretend that he does.

While most organizations have a purpose statement, a vision statement, or mission statement, very few have the clarity of vision, purpose, or mission to guide their decisions and actions. Ironically, the fashion of constructing statements can work against a true sense of vision, purpose, and mission, because often the statements end up being compromises on the part of people who write them. The statements have usually trivialized the organization's most meaningful concepts through weak, watered-down, simplistic declarations. This is due in part to a technical flaw in the approach that organizations commonly use.

Teams of people sit in rooms at off-site locations and consider the reasons they exist as an organization. They gain valuable insight and often begin to experience a sense of what might be described as the organization's higher calling. So far, so good. But then they are charged with the task of putting that *spirit* into the confines of one phrase, sentence, paragraph, or statement. This task would be hard for the world's greatest poets, let alone those who are relatively inexperienced in translating complex ideas into words.

The resulting statement usually tells us little about the unifying principles that will guide the organization's strategies and policies. Often it is awkward and vague:

> We are the company that has the most advanced technology in widget design, is recognized for being the industry leader in quality, has high market share with totally satisfied loyal customers, in an environment where people are able to develop their talents and abilities by meeting the challenges of today and tomorrow, while producing extremely high profitability.

Which would we rather work for, a company that had a purpose statement but didn't have a purpose, or a company that had a purpose but didn't have a purpose statement? Of course we would all choose reality over mannerism. But even an organization that has a true purpose can rob that purpose of its power by reducing it to a slogan.

When I consult with clients, we don't talk a lot about their purpose. That is not to say the topic is absent from our work together. Far from it. It just is not talked about very much.

It comes up, though, when we talk about the work the organization does, what the organization could be, the values that employees want to live by, and the aspirations they have for it. It also is seen by what disappoints these people and what they regret. We see it in their hope for the company, and their frustrations with it. We see it in their desire for the future, and their pride in their past accomplishments. We see it in the love they have for their organization.

Without a clear sense of the organization's purpose, we would not be able to design the company, because how can we design something that has no apparent point?

Of course, some things are better off *not* said. Not because they should be hidden, but because as soon as you try to say them, they seem somehow less than they truly are. Sometimes, words just can't do justice to some of the most important qualities in life, like the deeper purpose of the organization.

Once in a while, a few people try to deny this aspect of their organizations. They may say, "Our purpose is return on investment," or, "Profit," or "Enhancing shareholders' value." They try to mean it when they say it. But we can put it to the test. Does the purpose truly serve the "profit motive"? Is that truly the organization's *prime* reason to exist, or just the way viability is created? If we took the same investment the organization represents, and put the money in a high-yield account, would we do better in terms of profit? Often, the answer is yes. Even when the answer is no, there are usually other ways to make more profit more easily.

Nevertheless, of the people who claim that return on investment is the purpose, they do not sell the company and put the money in a bank, or some other form of investment. While money is a considerable factor, it is hardly ever the fundamental reason the organization exists.

There is in each of us a dynamic urge to build, grow, aspire, and create. Not all of us have this urge to the same intensity. Not all of us have the same desires or aspirations. But we surely can observe that we possess such deep urges.

We would rather be doing something important than something unimportant. We would rather be involved with something that matters, than with something that doesn't.

At their root, most organizations have something special, something quite human. It is the highest manifestation of the human spirit to join together to do something that matters. And when that spirit is granted its place in the scheme of things, we are ready to do our work.

Advancement, Not Oscillation

Structural oscillation is characterized by the dominance of various structural conflicts. Structural advancement is characterized by the dominance of structural tension as the unifying thematic principle within the organization. We want structural tension, and we don't want structural conflict. Our design work must be based on structural tension, for if it isn't we will tend to find ourselves in an oscillating pattern.

The fundamental structural tension upon which the organization may be built—its unifying principle—is formed by the desired state (the full expression of the organization's purpose) in relationship to the actual state (the current expression of its purpose). This prime structural tension can form the basis for all other goals, strategies, policies, decisions, and actions of the organization (see next page).

The desired organizational purpose answers this question: Why do we exist as an organization? Unlike most goals, the purpose of an organization is ongoing. We can't put a due date on it, bring it in on time, and then sit back in satisfaction. The purpose is a constant force at play within the organization because it is *the* basic motivation for the organization to exist.

Singleness of purpose is rare in an organization. There are many other motives people have, both personally and professionally. The primary organizational purpose can get lost, particularly if it is contradicted by the organization's actions. When inconsistency of

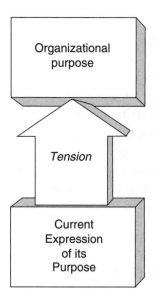

purpose exists, people begin to look for other motivations to do their jobs. Therefore it is important for an organization to sort out its purpose and use it as the thematic unifying principle throughout the organization.

While the purpose may be difficult to articulate, nonetheless it can be discussed. And it can be felt. Members of an organization usually have a natural affinity to the organization's true purpose so, while it may be hard to talk about, they can recognize it.

Rather than relying on slogans, one powerful way to communicate the purpose to members of the organization is by managerial actions, decisions, strategies, and policies that are consistent with it. Actions do speak louder than words.

Once the desired purpose is established, the next step is to observe the current reality: What is the actual current expression of the purpose? Some days we will express the purpose of the organization more consistently than other days, but we certainly can see the general trends and patterns.

This form of structural tension between the desired and current purpose is *generative*. When this structural tension becomes the dominant force, it will be reinforced throughout the organization. This will lead to structural advancement rather than structural oscillation. Now we come to the fifth law of organizational structure.

THE FIFTH LAW OF ORGANIZATIONAL STRUCTURE

> # When structural tension dominates an organization, the organization will advance.

This fifth law of organizational structure holds the key to structural advancement. When structural tension is the dominant force in the organization (when the unifying principle penetrates the organization), all key members of the organization are aware of the desired state in their area, and the organization's current state of reality in relationship to the goals. Not only that, but each member is aware of how local goals fit other departmental and organizational goals, and how the parts fit together to form a comprehensive strategy. People are focused on a collective vision of the company, and they are fluent in recognizing reality at any given moment. They are building structural tension together by doing their part within the well-structured whole. Mistakes and success are part of the learning process that enable the organization to increase its capacity to fulfill its purpose.

In an organization where structural tension is the dominant structure, a structural approach is built in companywide. Swedforest, an international forestry consulting company with headquarters in Sweden, is such an organization. Jerker Thunberg, Swedforest's managing director, recently talked about his company's experience with using the structural approach:

> During the two years Swedforest has worked with structural approach, most of our staff and managers, as well as administrative and support staff, have been involved in defining what we want to be and what results we want to achieve. The structural approach, building strategies taking you toward the desired results, is an enormously powerful tool for change and management. The realization of the structural tension between desired end results and current reality has given us energy to start changing the organization to achieve the results we want.

Swedforest is not the same company as it was two years ago and the most fascinating and positive thing is that once you start working with the structural approach there is no way back to the old problem-solving, situational thinking that is so self-defeating. We become more and more effective and successful. I can only wish that many more companies will start to learn and apply a structural approach in managing themselves.

The Self-Organizing System

Not only is structural tension something that must be established consciously, but it also takes meticulous reinforcement throughout the organization so that all the local levels support the broader organizational design. What kinds of organizing systems are required to accomplish this? Must they be strict, tight, and rigid? Not at all.

People from all levels need the latitude to do their jobs. They need to use their best judgment, they need to be able to manage their mandates. But they must also be given mandates that support the highest interests of the organization. There must be a common direction.

With so much interest these days in self-organizing management systems, can structural tension be established and supported by such a system? This is a crucial question for companies that are exploring the premise of chaos theory, complexity, and self-organization.

Because it takes great diligence to create structural tension as the prime force within an organization, we can predict self-organizing management systems most often will not work. Instead they will tend to produce oscillating behavior as local forces gain strength and power, only to clash with other local forces.

Chaos, Complexity, and Order

We sit in the concert hall, awaiting the arrival of the conductor. The musicians wander on stage and take their seats. Eventually, there are more than one hundred players warming up their instruments and fingers, tuning, practicing especially difficult passages, adjusting their reeds or strings or mouthpieces or seats or music stands. The hundred individuals perform thousands of acts that are uncoordinated and random. No moment is exactly like another, and individual chance events join with other individual chance events to form a *predictable* state of cacophony. (Chance events notwithstanding, when it is tuning, every orchestra sounds like every other orchestra.)

An orchestra tuning is a *self-organizing system*; in other words, it is a *complex* created by incalculable numbers of occurrences that are self-generated and self-arranged. There is no plan to the multitude of events that occur, but they form predictable and consistent sound patterns.

What can we say about this organization? In many ways, a tuning orchestra fulfills many of the important criteria often described as essential to organizational success:

- It has a common purpose (to tune each instrument to a common pitch).

- Each individual takes personal responsibility for fulfilling that purpose.

- Each member is a highly trained professional, fully capable of performing any task required.

However, this organization, the orchestra, is predictably limited in its ability to produce music within the self-organizing system that tuning produces. When we listen to an orchestra tuning up, we can recognize it for what it is. We do not confuse the tuning with the music about to be performed. If the evening consisted of hours of musicians tuning, we would justifiably want our money back.

But after a short time the musicians become quiet. The conductor comes to the podium. The baton is raised, and with the first downbeat the musicians produce music that is far more interesting, structurally and emotionally complex, dramatic, and moving, than any sounds that came from the orchestra when they were tuning.

We have witnessed a transformation from unharnessed potential that reached a status quo to focused potential fulfilling its promise. What made the difference? Not talent, dedication, skill, professionalism, resources, energy, and attention to detail, for there was no change in these characteristics.

In business, we often hear the call for more of these very qualities. "Our organization needs more dedication, attention to detail, a higher skill level, more professionalism, more resources, more energy."

These certainly are useful and important qualities to have in an organization. But, as we can see from our orchestral example, by themselves these factors are not enough. The composer and the conductor provide vision, leadership, and a profound understanding of structure that enables the resources of the orchestra to be put to good use.

The musical score is the most dominant factor. An orchestra with a conductor but without a score would hardly be more productive than the tuning-up exercise. In fact an orchestra can play a score without a conductor, although usually not as well. So the composer's role is supreme.

But the best score, unperformed, does not reach its height of fulfillment either. The composer, the conductor, and each musician performs a unique function within the musicmaking process. The separation of function allows each individual to serve the performance of the music. At its best, the orchestra is one of the finest examples of organizational control—the ability of a group of people to join together and accomplish their collective purpose through their shared efforts. Control is multiplied throughout the organization by combining clarity of a unifying principle (score) with competence of personnel (musicians) and leadership skills (conductor).

An organization can be as highly professional as the world's best orchestras once it becomes well-structured, with a thematic unifying principle that is consistently reinforced throughout its various activities. To learn the lesson of the orchestra, we must move away from self-organizing systems that produce limited status-quo results and into a highly composed system that is capable of superior performance.

Quick Review

- An organization is not an organic phenomenon of nature. It is a refined human invention.

- Activities are usually tied together by a common cause or purpose.

- Organizations have the advantage and disadvantage of being divided into sections.

- It takes good structural design work to tie the parts of the organization together.

- In the arts, the factor that ties the parts together is called the thematic unifying principle, a factor that can be used in organizations.

- A telltale sign of the lack of a unifying principle is an inconsistent decision-making process.

- Mission, purpose, and vision statements do not serve to tie an organization together because they trivialize the most meaningful principles of the organization.

- Most organizations have a real purpose. Too often this purpose is not used as a thematic unifying principle in designing the organization.

- The fundamental organizational structural tension is the relationship between the organization's purpose and the current expression of that purpose.

- The fifth law of organizational structure is: **When structural tension dominates an organization, it will advance.**

- It takes consciously conceived design and discipline, leadership, learning, and structural understanding, to make structural tension dominant within an organization.

- Self-organizing management systems will tend to lead to oscillating patterns, because structural conflicts will become dominant.

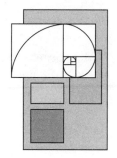

CHAPTER 8

Structural Tension and the Business Strategy

An organization's *purpose* is its thematic unifying principle, its cornerstone, its foundation. How do we build the organization upon it? How do we support it? How do we reinforce the principle throughout the organization so that structural tension dominates and the organization advances?

The first step is to make the organization viable, so that its purpose can be fulfilled. This is done through its business strategy.

Defining Business Strategy

Purpose is expressed through the organization as a business that funds the enterprise. The business strategy answers the question, how does the organization generate wealth? How does it generate its own viability?

An organization's purpose forms the desired state for the prime structural tension that drives the organization. This tension is the most senior, and so all else emanates from it.

Since tension seeks resolution, the actual state (the current expression of the purpose) moves toward the desired state (the fulfillment of the purpose) through the business strategy, which is the action that resolves the tension:

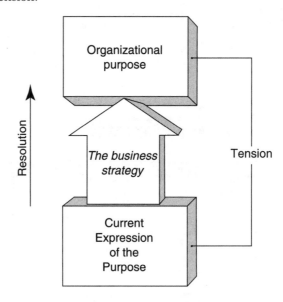

Whereas business strategy describes how the organization generates wealth (how it makes money), a management strategy describes how work gets done through the coordination of various resources (people, systems, machines). Business and management are distinct disciplines that require different sets of skills and abilities. When this distinction is not made, the function of each discipline becomes obscure, and policies are often designed with built-in structural conflicts between competing forces.

When this distinction is truly made, management strategy serves the business strategy, which serves the purpose.

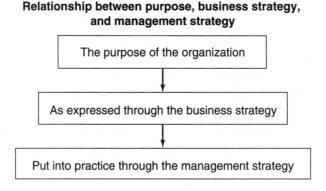

Relationship between purpose, business strategy, and management strategy

A company that competes for market share will spawn a different business strategy than one that develops a small niche in a larger market. If a company brings new products to market, investment in product development may be essential in the business design. Wealth may be generated by its investment strategies, and therefore economic tactics will be closely designed and managed. If quality of service is essential in a market, quality sensitivity becomes part of the business strategy.

Many organizations adopt a shotgun approach to their business strategy: "Let's do it all! If one thing is good, then more are better!" Product development, niche markets, financial investment, and total quality are all considered equally viable. However, a built-in deficiency of shotgun strategies is that they weaken organizational critical thinking. If *everything* is good, than individual elements of a strategy become arbitrary. Relationships between various factors are dulled, and everything is made to compete for the same resource base. Resources are squandered. Actions cancel out other actions.

An Exercise in Business Strategy

In some of our training sessions, we help managers develop their strategic business skills by dividing the participants into two groups and giving each group a business scenario. For example, both groups may be told that they are in the microchip business, but one group will be in the commodities end of the industry, while the other group will be in the designer-boutique microchip market. This would be the only information given the two groups, and then they are allowed twenty minutes to develop a business strategy.

Frequently, the people in each group spend their time in *managerial*, rather than *business*, discussions.

Often goals have been created that show no understanding of or relationship to how their group's company makes money. Typically, people say things like "We will increase sales 25 percent next year." "We will dominate our market internationally." "We will increase our profit margin to a 23% return on investment." Extraordinarily, these goals have been created in a vacuum. (Increase, compared to what? Return of investment, in relationship to what?)

When participants are asked what they were attempting to

accomplish with these types of goals, they aren't able to answer. They don't really know.

Many participants did not think of the business strategy as how the organization generates wealth. In their own companies they had used the term *business strategy* to describe the process by which to achieve certain types of goals.

During their own planning meetings, many managers had created goals by extrapolating increases or decreases from their previous year's performance: 10 percent more of this, 15 percent less of that. More sales . . . more productivity . . . less overhead . . . less cost.

These goals do not reflect an understanding of how the business actually works. In fact, these types of goals are often designed to help people do just a little better than they did last year.

Once managers write these types of goals on their flip charts, their next question is "How are we going to get there?" They may call this process "business strategy. " It's not truly *strategic*, because it doesn't reflect anything *generative*. At best, it might be tactical. But a set of tactics without a strategy doesn't have much of a point. It just reminds us of the old joke: "Strategic planning, the way most companies do it, is neither."

Some managers in our microchip exercise were in the habit of forming business goals that were merely an extrapolation of past performance. "If we sold 20,000 units last year, let's sell 20 percent more this year." Some of them used popular clichés of the day: "We will develop our core competencies," or "We will have total quality," or "We will be customer focused." As we explored the reasoning behind their thought processes, it became clear that no one could build a business based on their approach.

How are we to think about business strategy? If we are in the microchip business, one important question might be this: What *motivates* the customer to buy our products or services? This is how we can begin to think in terms of a real business strategy.

Many companies do too much self-referential thinking about their customers, a common mistake. They tend to see customers from their own, rather than the customer's, point of view.

"Why would your customers buy from you?" we might ask. "Because we have value added," or "Because we have the most variety," or "Because we have the capability to deliver any time of day."

Added value is not the reason customers really make their buying decisions, but rather *value* itself. Added value is often a rationale suppliers use to justify their price. How much variety a company has is irrelevant to a customer who only wants one item. An organization's capability to deliver anytime is not the reason most customers buy. They only care if they can get the product or service when they want it.

The phrase "customer focus" has a lovely ring to it. However, it doesn't answer this important question: What *motivates* the customer to buy? This question leads us to a different orientation in our understanding of customers. We can put ourselves in the customers' shoes and attempt to understand their concerns and values. How and why does the customer actually make buying decisions?

Because they have surveyed customers, defined customers' needs, evaluated the competition, put TQM into the organization, and developed their customer-service department, many people think they are totally customer focused. But too often, in spite of these valuable practices, the customer's true motivation remains obscure. This is why people can be surprised when, after so much "customer focus," the customer decides to go elsewhere.

In our exercise, we gave the groups a chance to rethink the microchip scenario. But this time, instead of a customer focus approach, we encouraged a customer motivation orientation.

Our Commodities Microchip Strategy

Why would a customer want to buy our product? Within the commodities end of the business, customers buy from their suppliers for two reasons: The products are *available* when they want them, and the product is *inexpensive*. Quality is not a factor *as long as quality is adequate*.

Customers want the price to be low so they can lower the price of their own products, making them more competitive in the marketplace. Customers want on-time, scheduled deliveries so they can meet their production timetables. *Available* and *inexpensive* leads to a network, or "tapestry," of other decisions: where manufacturing plants should be built, how transport and delivery systems should be organized, how costs and pricing should be determined. Therein lie the beginnings of a solid business strategy.

Would we build our manufacturing plants in places where the cost of living is high? No. We would build them where the cost of living is low. Would we build them in a place where there are high labor costs? No. We would look for places where there is inexpensive labor, but where the labor force can be competent, professional, and consistent. Would we build off-shore? Perhaps, if the country had the right combination of cost and available competent labor. We would also look for places where there is political stability. Perhaps we would look for other advantages, such as good tax benefits and local investment in our plants.

As we think about our costs, we must also consider transport. What are the transport costs now? What will they be in the future? We want a plant we can utilize for a very long time, so we would need to study factors that influence its longevity. What is the history of potential sites?

What are current trends? What can be reasonably predicted for the future? What might we *not* be able to predict? Would what we can't predict put us at undue risk? If so, why should we take the risk? Perhaps we need to find a more suitable location that enjoys similar advantages but has less potential risk involved.

What about availability of our products to our customers? How do we ship? Do we have local warehouses, local distribution? Since there are two major factors involved—price and availability—both must be successfully accommodated.

There are other factors as well, one of which is reputation. But reputation must be based on reality: Can we actually deliver the microchips our customers want, at the right price, at the right time? No matter how good our reputation is, it will deteriorate rapidly if we don't "deliver the goods."

We may also need to update our microchips to meet our customers' need for their future products, so we might have a product development division. On the other hand, we might prefer to arrange licensing agreements with other companies to avoid the overhead, something that would drive our costs up. If we license or buy new microchips when they enter the commodity realm, we can limit our costs and stay competitive.

If we were able to make this offer to our customer, would they be likely to say yes:

We can supply you with the microchips you want at the level of quality you want and the lowest cost, and get them to you when you want them with the least amount of hassle. In addition, when you need the next generation of microchips, we will have them for you at the lowest cost, etc.

If you were the customer, it would be hard to say no to that offer. Part of our marketing job is to tell the story accurately so potential customers know it is true.

The Designer Microchip Strategy

The strategy for the designer-boutique microchip end of the industry would be quite different. Why do customers buy these chips? Our customers are making new high-tech products themselves. They need to meet product-development schedules, since time to the market is one of the most important factors in determining their success. They need microchips that meet their specs, perform reliably, and must be delivered on time. Innovation, design, and quality of engineering are acutely important. Since these chips are custom tailored to be used in specialized products, price sensitivity is less important than unique design.

Our customer's buying decision would be based on two major factors: *quality of innovation* and *timeliness*. Therefore, this would be the basis for our business strategy.

One of the demands of the strategy is to have exceptionally talented engineers, technologists, and computer scientists. How do we get them? We would make our company the most attractive in the industry. We would pay the highest salaries. We would locate our facilities in "lifestyle" areas that have an excellent standard of living, very good schools, good weather, and so on. We might also think about locating near a major university such as MIT or Stanford. We might recruit future talent by scouting the high-school science fairs. We would certainly head-hunt in the best colleges and universities. By attracting the most talented people to our organization, we develop a capacity for innovation that is exceedingly meaningful to our customers. The other factor is timeliness. To assure timeliness, we would use the same strategy and apply it to managerial talent. We would want the best technical managers we could get, people who could work with our group of superstar technologists.

How would our potential customers know we could produce the innovation they need, reliably and on time? Our marketing approach would emphasize our track record. We might also use a "worth by association" tactic: Perhaps we would hire several Nobel Prize winners to serve on our advisory board, or even invite them into a special think tank. This would help us tell our story to the world: reliable innovation.

The boutique end of the microchip business is not price sensitive. Therefore, we need to structure our pricing policies high enough to support our cost structure.

Conflicts of Strategies

Each business strategy generates a tapestry of related decisions. If managers in the organization are not cognizant of the strategy, they might fail to support it properly. If they are, then they have a greater ability to relate the parts to the whole. Once we come to understand the importance of a true business strategy, and then develop one of our own, the criteria for decisions comes into sharp focus. We can make decisions quickly and wisely. We can put them into practice easily, for each decision reinforces other decisions, and our unity of direction builds momentum.

This microchip business scenario comes from the real world. The company in question wanted both a commodities and a designer microchip business. But they attempted to fuse these two different businesses into one.

Why did they fail to see the distinction between the two? Partly it happened because they had built a large plant at an enormous expense. Once they had built it, they wanted to use it for both businesses to justify their original decision to build the plant. As one decision led to another, the factors each microchip business strategy required were compromised. This made it harder to compete in either business against companies that had realized the nature of the industry and what motivated the customer.

To make matters worse, the commodities and designer microchip divisions were forced to compete against each other for the same resource base. This was due to a structural conflict that developed between attempts to cut costs on the one hand and build the business on the other. Leadership lost its direction, but attempted to regain control by issuing directives that made no sense from a business point of view: "We want 40 percent of our business to come from designer microchips." Where they came up with the 40 percent remains a mystery to this day.

It is hard to create a good argument in favor of being less effective than we can be. But, as structural conflicts dominate an organization, the direction can seem lost and effectiveness be diminished.

Organizations need to support their purpose through their business strategy. Not only that, the business strategy must be rethought regularly. Leaders, in particular, need to stay in touch with the strategy as an ongoing factor. The business strategy is the basis of structural tension.

Organizational purpose

Business strategy

Current state of business strategy

Current state of purpose

Unless a company understands the fundamentals of its business strategy, it will be unable to design consistent and productive management strategies. And without a business strategy, it will be unable to use structural tension to create an organization that advances.

How to Develop a Business Strategy

Based on my consulting work with organizations, I have developed the following questions to help guide an organization to construct a business strategy:

- What is our offering?
- Who are our customers?
- What do they want?
- What do we want?
- Is there a match between their wants and ours?
- How do they know about us?
- How do they obtain our offering?
- What is the current market?
- What is the future market?
- How will our offerings change?
- Where are we going?

Each question helps illuminate a vital area in our thinking process.

What Is Our Offering?

What do we actually offer our customers? One company offered customers various plastic-tray products. But, as we further explored the subject with this organization, we found their plastic trays were used by customers to shrink wrap their retail products. While continuing to sell the plastic trays to many of its customers, the company had begun to develop a new offering: the entire packaging process as a service. They had developed the capacity to take a customer's product, package it, shrink wrap it, box it, and drop ship it. This proved to be a more attractive offering to their customers.

In this example, the organization has the potential to offer its customers more than plastic trays. They can take the burden of packaging and shipping processes off of their customers' shoulders. They can take away some of their customers' overhead and fixed costs. If the company manages its organization strategically, they can do a better job than their customers and do it for less money. That is an offering many companies would find it hard to turn down. It is a great offering.

Who Are Our Customers?

Often organizations presume to know who their customers are because it seems so self-evident, and often their presumption is correct. However, when designing a business strategy, it is essential to rethink this question. Sometimes the customer is neither the funder nor the user of the product or service. Managed health care organizations, for example, have users (the patients), funders (the insurance companies), and customers (the HMOs themselves). We need to determine who is who in such an industry. Who influences and who makes the buying decisions? This leads to our next question.

What Do They Want?

What motivates our potential customers to make the decisions they make? From their point of view, what is in their best interests? What are their values, and what do they value? What are they looking for, and why? (This key point should not be underestimated, for a major dimension to our business strategy will be based on what motivates the customer.)

What Do We Want?

The sales force has just proudly landed a big contract. They get big commissions. Suddenly the new workload strains the company's capacity to a point where it is hard to fulfill regular orders. People debate whether we should have taken the new contract. Even as the debate goes on, the enterprising sales force is drumming up more big contracts. We could be in trouble.

Our activities must be consistent with our real aspirations and strategies. An organization can lose its way when it doesn't know what it wants. It can choose to engage in projects it doesn't care about; or projects that are good from a short-term perspective but bad from a long-term perspective. For example, when people can enhance their own compensation by committing the organization to activities that do not support the organization's direction, the reward system may reinforce *disorganization*.

A company should not really be "customer driven." Instead, it should possess its own sense of direction, identity, purpose, and strategy. Without knowing what we want, we might harm ourselves by trying to be all things to everyone. We need to stay in touch with what motivates us.

What Is the Match Between the Customer's Wants and Ours?

Once we know what motivates the customer and what motivates us, the question is, what is the match? When there is a strong match, we have the basis for doing business. We can build relationships with customers based on mutuality, so that transactions are in everyone's best interest. We can build a comprehensive business strategy that works and gathers momentum.

How Do They Know About Us?

It is not enough to have the best product in the industry. We may have the greatest mouse trap in the world, but if no one knows about it the path to our door will be overgrown with weeds. The market must know we have the best product and that it is in their best interest to buy it.

Market research may be useful, but often it gives us mixed signals. If we are not looking for a match between what we do, what we offer, what the market wants, and what motivates our customers' decisions, we can be misled by market research.

Marketing is its own art and, perhaps, science. However, whatever the methods adopted, the organization must make sure its marketing approach is consistent with its purpose, business strategy, style, values, products, scope, and so on.

In a way, everything that touches the customer is marketing. Consideration must be given to the way we write letters, answer the phone, serve needs, handle complaints, and anticipate future aspirations. A thematic unifying strategy helps to focus marketing, so there is a consistent message whenever a customer is in contact with us.

Good marketing will accomplish several essential objectives. It will tell our potential customers who we are, what we do, how we do it, and what the match is between us. It will also keep the match between our current customers and ourselves visible, so they will continue to be aware of that match.

How Do They Obtain Our Offering?

Once customers know about our offering and want it, how do they get it? How do we distribute it? It is essential that distribution systems be thought through with care. Delays in delivery can hurt. So can the wrong cost structure; distribution costs must fit into the overall economic strategy, particularly in price-sensitive markets.

What Is the Current Market?

This aspect of our business strategy gives us the opportunity to rethink our built-in assumptions. Perhaps our market is wider or narrower than we think. If either is true, what are the implications to our business strategy? Perhaps the current market can include another entire segment we hadn't considered before. Perhaps we need to target our potential customers with an accurate profile of the best customers we currently have, so we can focus our marketing efforts toward those most likely to buy.

What Is the Future Market?

Markets change. To what degree can we anticipate what the future will be? If we are a strong player in our market, we might be able to drive the future. If we aren't, we might lose our market to smaller competitors who are more visionary and sensitive to the times. Both Wang and Microsoft have been the strongest force in their respective markets. As we all know, Wang once owned the word-processing market, but lost it when they did not stay current. As market leaders, they did not drive the future; so, without intending to, they left that to others.

Microsoft, on the other hand, does drive the future in its market. They do so, not because they always have the best software products, but because they are very clear about what they want, what the customers want, and what the match is. They understand their offering is not simply products, or systems of products that are compatible;

they offer ease of use from the customer's point of view and experience. They are very aware of what motivates the customer, so they can easily anticipate future trends and invest in technological development that will be relevant in the future. When they are not driving development, they employ an aggressive acquisition strategy that buys out any potentially serious competitor. They do not take their position for granted. They constantly rethink their business strategy so they are always current.

Both Sony and Kodak are anticipating the future in the world of filmmaking. The approaches they are taking are indicative of what they want as companies. Kodak is driving technological advances in film stocks, making them easier to use under any lighting condition. Currently, film looks much better visually than video. On the other hand, video has some advantages that Kodak is attempting to duplicate within the medium of film. Kodak is working in a chemical world, whereas Sony is working in an electronic world. The dream of many filmmakers is to have electronic film: the look of real film with the convenience of an electronic digital domain. As long ago as 1941, Orson Welles said to John Tolland, his famous cinematographer, "Isn't it a shame the film has to be in the camera." Welles was anticipating the day when film was made with an "electric eye" that would be more maneuverable. Sony is experimenting with high-definition digital video and "filmizing" techniques that make video look like film. It may be impossible for Sony to succeed, because the nature of chemical film media has a certain look to it—rich texture, depth, color, tonality, and so on. But if they succeed, Sony will own the electronic "film" market in the future.

How Will Our Offerings Change?

Ten years ago, Kodak's film stocks were engineered very differently than they are today. The new film stocks are easier to use, and can be used under a wider set of conditions. Kodak has done a superb job of perfecting the new super-16 format, used widely for television dramas and even feature films. Before the 16-mm format was perfected, most television was shot on the more expensive 35-mm format.

Who drives change, the market or the market leaders? Each industry will have its own answer, but as we build our business strategy we need to anticipate how our offering will change. Change is not just more of the same. It can be an entirely different approach to the customer. Good strategy is not something written in stone and then enforced by rigid rules. It is alive, dynamic.

Where Are We Going?

Often organizations can become so myopic that while they obsess about details they lose touch with overall trends and patterns. An organization needs a sense of the future. If we think tomorrow will look like today, we are out of touch with reality. It will not. We need to know where we want to go—what our desired state is—and our current state in relationship to our desired state.

By answering the preceding questions, we can forge a true business strategy that supports our purpose. The strategy can then be turned into structural tension, which in turn can translate into a managerial approach. These straightforward questions help us focus on:

- What we should do
- How we should do it
- How it will work (viability)
- Where we are going

Everyone who makes decisions within an organization benefits from understanding the overall design of the enterprise. This *meta-dimension* helps organize decisions into consistent frames. Local levels of the organization can be arranged to support more senior levels of the structure.

In the next chapter, we will discuss how using structural tension in a business strategy changes the organization's behavior and leads to its advancement.

Quick Review

- The organization creates viability through its business strategy, which answers the question: How does the company generate wealth?

- Business strategy expresses the purpose of the organization and defines how wealth is generated. The management strategy puts the business strategy into practice by defining how work gets done through the coordination of people, systems, and other resources.

- Managers too often do not understand the company's business strategy, and therefore make decisions that ultimately conflict with it.

- The purpose of the organization is expressed through the business strategy, which is then put into practice through the management strategy.

- Shotgun approaches to business strategies cost too much and leave the organization unfocused and undisciplined.

- The term *business strategy* sometimes has been used to describe the process by which simple increases in performance are attempted. This use of the term does not tell us how the company generates wealth and is not a true business strategy.

- Once a business strategy is established, it leads to a tapestry of related decisions.

- The best way to develop a business strategy is to answer these questions:

  – What is our offering?

  – Who are our customers?

  – What do they want? What do we want?

  – Is there a match between our wants and theirs?

  – How do they know about us?

  – How do they obtain our offering?

  – What is the current market? The future market?

  – How will our offerings change?

  – Where are we going?

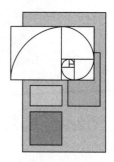

CHAPTER 9

Change of Structure

Two Faces of the Organization

The modern organization is capable of accomplishing something quite extraordinary. It can be a vehicle for expressing that which is highest in the human spirit—our inclination to build, invent, explore, learn, and create. It harnesses the power of vast resources into a collective force, turning great vision into reality. It saves lives through scientific research and development, helps the world communicate through technology, and generates then distributes wealth through industry. It is a vital, civilizing force.

Yet the organization also has its darker side. Sometimes it seems like an impersonal bureaucracy, capable of tearing peoples' lives apart, as has happened time and time again with the advent of downsizing. Chronic inefficiency squanders money, time, and talent. Political intrigues lead people to work against each other. Short-sightedness can defeat the organization's vision and purpose, and limit its success. The organizational hold on reality sometimes weakens to a point where no one seems to know, or even wants to know, what is going on.

111

Given these very different faces of the organization, what is its future? Can the organization really change?

Structure and Behavior

Without an understanding of structure, well-meaning people attempt to change their organization by adopting the popular approaches that are available to them. However, the change effort typically attempts to change behavior or process systems. The underlying organizational structure is left unaddressed.

Changing Behavior

When faced with inadequate structures, our natural tendency is to develop and employ compensating strategies; we try to find ways around the inadequacies. If the wheels of our car were out of alignment and pulled to the left, to drive straight we would compensate by steering to the right. Some might suggest a *behavioral* change: "You keep pulling the steering wheel to the right. Now, we've done many studies on the steering performances of successful drivers, and we find successful drivers steer straight when they are driving straight. So, if you want to be like other successful drivers, what you should do is steer in a straight line!"

We might take their advice, only to find we could not sustain it for long. The underlying structure of our car would not adapt to a change of behavior, it would not suddenly travel straight when we steered it straight. Instead, it would pull to the left even more than when we were compensating by steering to the right. Our car cannot do anything but perform as it does. The new strategy makes matters worse, and we will need to compensate with radical measures, suddenly steering to the right again if we are to avoid an accident. *Attempting to change our behavior when the underlying structure does not support the change only makes matters worse.* This leads us to the sixth law of structure.

THE SIXTH LAW OF ORGANIZATIONAL STRUCTURE

> # If the organization's structure remains unchanged, the organization's behavior will revert to its previous behavior.

This sixth law of organizational structure is quite revealing. *Any* change effort that does not address the underlying structural make-up of an organization will not work; the organization will simply revert to the way it behaved before the change effort. Without a change in underlying structure, the organization *must* fall into previous patterns. This is an inescapable law of organizational structure.

Organizations typically attempt to change behavior without under-standing the real cause for current behavior. Members of the organi-zation are asked to adopt new concepts, beliefs, and actions. Decrees for proper behavior are promoted in the form of "value statements" or "codes." The Achilles' heel of these approaches is a notion that the way people act within organizations is based primarily on their own individual choices. In fact, they usually are responding to other forces in play, structural forces that are not of the individual's own making: conflicting rewards and penalties, conflicting loyalties, unclear direc-tion, mixed messages, and so on.

If we could merely prescribe new behaviors for members of an organization, life would be a lot simpler. Instead, we need to deter-mine why people act in predictable ways. Unless we understand the causes of their behavior, we cannot hope to improve it.

Changing Process Systems

Just as some people mistakenly try to change the organization by changing people's behavior, others try to change the process system.

A change of process system, in our car analogy, might lead others to give us a different sort of advice: "To steer straight, first look down the road, then pull the wheel to the left, then to the right, and then, quickly to the left again . . ." Initially we might become more efficient at executing our new strategy, but later we will return to the same behavioral tendency—to steer to the right when we want to drive straight. The sixth law of structure applies here as well. The structure has not changed, so the behavior will not change.

Organizations change systems and procedures in the hope that they will change prevailing unproductive behavioral patterns. However a system adopted for the wrong reason is doomed from the start. Michael Greenidge, a business process design manager for BC Telecom, described this situation that many organizations experience:

> Every time we go through some major organizational change, our executive managers find "tools" or methods to help. ABCM, reengineering, different process consultants bring in other methods—we implement them, but then we find half way through the process the organization isn't taking them on. So then we abandon them, but later new tools are brought in. People are really up in the air about it all.

Is it any wonder that people easily slip into the role of house skeptics? Over the years, many have watched change effort after change effort hit their organizations, and have seen excitement for each new system blossom but then fade once the idea is put into practice. They have seen champions, systems, and mottoes come and go while the organization remains unchanged. Their lack of enthusiasm for the next new system to come down the pike is based on a wealth of previous experience: change efforts consistently fail.

These people are forced to conclude that change efforts are wasteful, that they take people away from the company's real work, and that they may even be distracting and harmful. The January 1992 issue of the European journal *Training and Development* cites a study that reinforces this opinion:

> In their quest for quality, many European companies are actually damaging their chances of improving their services and competitiveness, according to the findings of a new report published by *The Economist* Intelligence Unit.
> The study, *Making Quality Work—Lessons from Europe's Lead-*

ing Companies was conducted by consultants and researchers from Ashridge Management College. George Binney, who led the study, says, "Total Quality Programs——company-wide, training-led, add-ons to existing jobs—are, at best, ineffective. At worst, they inoculate the organization against real change."

Binney is also scathing about the emphasis so many companies put on standards such as BS 5750 and ISO 9000. "They are the bureaucracy of quality," he says. "They have a useful role to play, but to start with the standards is to put the cart before the horse."

An Implication

There is a subtle assumption built into the way many organizations approach change—a devastating implication: Our reason to act is primarily *circumstantial*.

At first, perhaps, there seems to be nothing strange about this notion. Our earliest experiences have taught us to react or respond to the world.

As children, we were taught the "proper" responses to circumstances concerning our physical well-being: crossing streets safely, for example. We quickly learned to psych out any situation, particularly those concerning adults, and develop compensating strategies to achieve positive outcomes. But, too often, we suffered an arrested development from these experiences. We adopted the premise that our role in life is limited to compensating for changing circumstances. When we hold this assumption, we are trapped by circumstances. We can think only in terms of past or present situations. If we consider the future at all, it is only to anticipate how circumstances might change so we can organize our reactions and responses accordingly.

We suffer an enormous invisible loss from this limitation. We lose touch with our *generative* faculties—the ability to envision new and original possibilities, born within the depth of our aspirations, independent of the prevailing circumstances. We relinquish our ability to imagine, invent, explore, and bring into being creations that have never been thought of before, ones that would have been impossible to conceive if we were merely extrapolating from previous trends.

Changing Structure

If we took the car to a garage and got the wheels aligned, our steering habits would change immediately. When we wanted to drive straight, we would steer straight. And it wouldn't take any time to adopt the new behavior. In this analogy, *a change of structure leads to a change of behavior automatically and naturally*. This, in fact, is the seventh law of organizational structure.

THE SEVENTH LAW OF ORGANIZATIONAL STRUCTURE

> # A change of structure leads to a change of the organization's behavior.

How do we create such profound change in the underlying structure of an organization? By building structural tension and using it as the prime organizing principle throughout the company.

Hierarchical Structural Tension

The organization's purpose—the desired state—and its current reality are the prime unit of structural tension; all else comes from this. Secondary is the business strategy—another desired state—and its current reality. The next lower level is the management strategy and its current reality. The next lower levels are the various local or divisional strategies and their states of current reality. This organizing system is hierarchical (see the illustration at the top of the next page).

The term *hierarchy* has come on bad times of late. After years of hierarchical management, burdened with excessive levels of fragmentation, "stove pipes," and inflexible bureaucracies, people rejoiced with the coming of a more enlightened era in which more flexible

Organizational purpose ————————————————————

Business strategy ————————————————————

Management _____
strategy

Local strategies ————————————————

Current state of _____
local strategies

Current state of   _____
management strategy

Current state of
business strategy

Current state of purpose ————————————————————

management was put into place. But the organization actually needs a different type of hierarchy—not one based on position or power, but one based on function and utility.

All activities within an organization are important or they should be abandoned. Functional hierarchy does not presume significance, since every activity has its own significance. *Functional hierarchy establishes order among activities.* A senior level in a functional hierarchy gives direction to the next level down, which gives direction to the next level down, and so on. Decisions made at one level, must be consistent with the next level up, and so on, until we get to the most senior level of the purpose.

Gloria Cosgrove, director of regulatory training, and an in-house structural consultant for Boehringer Pharmaceutical, has described what it is like when this relational focus is present:

> From a management point of view, the people working with me are extremely focused in terms of where we are going and where we are. They were involved in the thought process, and, there is a very different energy in the group. They are all on the same track, and they really understand it. Not just the work, but they really understand the thought process—how things fit together, how they work as a whole—versus having some information typed up on a plaque that is only a bunch of words.

Stephen H. Dunn, (AVP) vice president, Service Management Products, for the Canadian Company NORTEL, talked about using structural tension within a business strategy, technology, and management partnership to build an integrated whole:

> We are partnering with a major telecommunications service provider in the USA to create a new Service Management Product. The partnership got off to a poor start as management decisions made on each side, based on individuals' perception of what was needed, created conflict and animosity which *led* to two separate teams with differing agendas rather than one with a common purpose. Using the principle of structural tension and applying it first to business and technology strategies has allowed us to clearly see the root cause of the situation we were in, and take appropriate action on management strategies. Our two separate teams are beginning to merge behind common goals, and decisions amongst the members now lead to real progress.

How functional hierarchy establishes order—how it becomes a unifying principle throughout the organization—can be illustrated with a case study.

South Tech's Story

South Tech, a start-up high-tech research and development organization, was developing a complex new hardware/software system, capable of bringing satellite technology to a new era of development[1]. The concept for their design is a product that connects various networks together—teleconferencing through cyberspace and satellite communications, and so on.

Their development had two aspects: to develop new technology that enabled many more systems and platforms to communicate (a technology that simply did not exist when they began their work), and to put this new technology into products.

The Key Business Strategy Decisions

There were two major factors that concerned South Tech: the quality of technological development, and the time required to reach the marketplace with their first release.

---

[1]In this example, the real company's name, industry, and strategy have been altered to hide its real identity. However, the example describes the thought process accurately.

These competing factors could form the basis of a structural conflict between market demands (which would drive quick development) and technological demands (which would drive a longer phase development time).

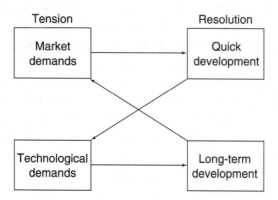

In fact, before structural tension was put into the organization as its dominant structure, discussions and debates would regularly surface about the real direction they should take. Should they hold off bringing the product to market until they had a more advanced version, or should they bring out a first-generation product without delay? The direction seemed to oscillate regularly. Decisions about direction, once made, seem to be unmade. And the debate went on.

South Tech needed a focused business strategy. How would the company generate wealth? One determinant was future market share. Because the market was clamoring for this type of product, the first company in the market with a useable product would have an enormous competitive advantage. The potential customers included some of the biggest companies in the world. The market was global. The stakes were high.

To be second or third in the market would weaken their position greatly. Then South Tech would be perceived as just a "me too" company. They would lose many major accounts and lose market share.

Not being first in the market was unacceptable to South Tech's leadership.

The other key competitive factor was the quality of the technology. Technologically, they were on an even playing field with their major competitors. No one had a distinct technological advantage.

Their concept of the product was full automation and integration with very little additional tech support needed. Given the choice between a "shrink wrap and ship" or a "send the product out with lots of tech support" scenarios, they preferred the former.

There were some key decisions to make in South Tech's business strategy—decisions that would define their functional hierarchy. South Tech's first decision was crucial to many other related decisions: they would emphasize an early time to market with a useable product.

Once South Tech decided that their key strategic factor was to be first in the market with a useable product that goal drove all others, including the quality of technology. If they were to be first, much of the engineering needed in a shrink-wrap-and-ship product would have to come later; therefore, they would need a secondary strategy to support the primary strategy of an early release. To assure the product could work well for their customers, they would need to create an intensive tech support system.

The First-Phase Strategy

The prime goal of the strategy, the first release date of their product, became the desired state of their first structural tension chart:

> Product X, version 1.0, is ready to ship
> with full production and distribution capacity
> by September (year 2 of project)

Now that the end result—the desired state—was defined and dated, the next step was to review current reality in relationship to it. This formed the prime architecture for the first structural tension chart (see the illustration at the top of the next page).

Action Plan—Part One

The next step after setting up the first structural tension framework is to develop the action plan. How do we move from the actual state to the desired state? South Tech's management group developed a strategy by asking this question: *What actions do we need to take?*

South Tech's management group studied the end result (the suc-

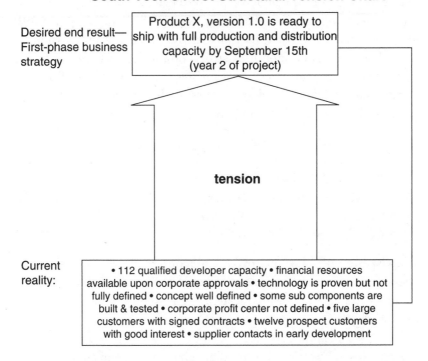

South Tech's First Structural Tension Chart

Desired end result—
First-phase business
strategy

| Product X, version 1.0 is ready to ship with full production and distribution capacity by September 15th (year 2 of project) |

tension

Current
reality:

• 112 qualified developer capacity • financial resources available upon corporate approvals • technology is proven but not fully defined • concept well defined • some sub components are built & tested • corporate profit center not defined • five large customers with signed contracts • twelve prospect customers with good interest • supplier contacts in early development

cessful release of their product) and the current reality, which included advantages, disadvantages, available resources, resources not yet available, and so on.

They were aware of the tension that existed between the desired state and the actual state. Because this tension is a dynamic force, it enabled them to "ride" the tension as a surfer might ride a wave. When we encounter tension, we want to resolve it. We want to take action on behalf of our desire, and so the tension aids us in our ability to write an action plan.

Action steps for the master structural tension chart are fairly broad. If they were any more detailed, we could miss the overview. Therefore, it is better to map out the action plan in broad strokes first and develop details later. Thus the actions that are put on the list locate the overview of the actions. We can design the shape of the action plan.

The action plan tells us what actual steps we will take, and where the major pivotal points are in our management strategy. However, the action plan does not exist in a state of abstract purity. As we become engaged in the action plan, we begin a more general organizational learning process called *progression*. Before we examine South Tech's action plan further, let's look at the process of progression.

When the organization uses structural tension as the basis for its management strategy, it builds a *progression—a movement from the current state to the desired state*. Within the organization, the progression develops the following characteristics over time:

- Consistency of motivation
- A repetition factor
- Continually increasing capability
- Continually increasing capacity
- Continually increasing effectiveness
- Consistency of motivation

Consistency of Motivation. Each action is clearly motivated and aligned with a consistent reason to act in the accomplishment of the business strategy (the desired state as expressed in the first structural tension chart).

A Repetition Factor. Rather than a hodge-podge of confusing and contradictory systems, we construct sensible procedures that can be used throughout the organization.

Continually Increasing Capability. Using a structural tension charting approach, we can more easily learn as we engage in the process. As current reality changes, we can learn from it. Over time, people in our organization can increase their skills and performance.

Continually Increasing Capacity. Our capacity can increase in many ways. The key is to anticipate capacity needs *before* new workload strains the organization. Structural tension charting helps us see where we might need to add people, systems, or other resources, so that we can bring them on line at the optimal time.

Continually Increasing Effectiveness. We do not learn the same lesson over and over. Learning is a cumulative process, and past learning becomes the foundation of new learning. For this reason, within a structural approach people increase their effectiveness over time and involvement.

The following illustration shows how the preceding characteristics are developed within the frame of structural tension as actions are taken.

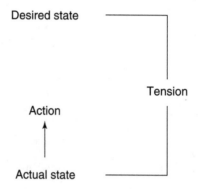

The action produces a consequence, or an immediate result:

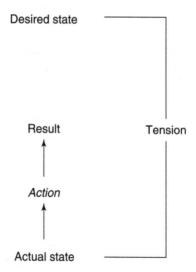

The result is evaluated from a perspective of structural tension. Did the action help the actual state move closer to the desired state?

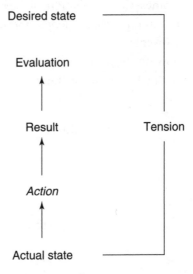

From our evaluation, we adjust our future actions:

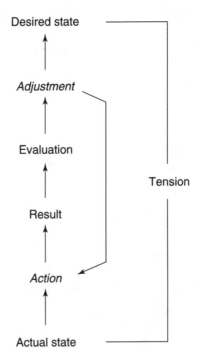

The cycle repeats itself until the desired outcome is achieved. As the cycle repeats, a change occurs. With each repetition, more is learned. Greater understanding and experience lead to greater effectiveness. We are able to take better actions producing better results, conduct better evaluations leading to better adjustments, and so on. The progression is in refining and strengthening the process while increasing capacity.

beginning capability ⎯⎯⎯⎯→ **more capable** ⎯⎯⎯⎯→

action–result–evaluation–adjustment–action–result–evaluation–adjustment–action–result–evaluation–

more capable ⎯⎯⎯⎯→ **more capable** ⎯⎯→

adjustment–action–result–evaluation–adjustment–action–result–evaluation–adjustment–action–result–

⎯⎯⎯⎯→ **more capable** ⎯⎯⎯⎯→

evaluation–adjustment–action–result–evaluation–adjustment–action–result–evaluation–adjustment–action

Action Plan—Part Two

The next step in South Tech's charting process was to list the major actions needed to accomplish the goal of releasing product X.

While using this process, there is no need to place action steps into a time line. South Tech's action steps were written on the list in the order they were conceived. A time frame would be established once they had listed all the steps.

As the list grew, South Tech's managers asked themselves this question: *If we took these actions, is it likely we would accomplish our goal?* Of course, they expected the answer to be no *until* they had listed all the essential actions needed to achieve the desired result, but asking the question helped focus their thoughts on the remaining steps.

Once they finished the action plan, they dated each action step in terms of completion (the due date, rather than the start date). Dating the actions organized them into a time frame (see "Structural Tension Chart: Business Strategy, Phase 1," on the next page).

Structural Tension Chart: Business Strategy, Phase 1

Product X, version 1.0, is ready to ship
with full production and distribution capacity
by September 15th (year 2 of project)

Action Item	Completion Date
Distribution channel is being fully satisfied	September 15 year 2
Customer feed back or difficulties on first releases have been corrected	August 15 year 2
First production run begins	June 15 year 2
Design and implement a customer service & maintenance program	November 15
	April 15 year 2
Customer and field testing completed on prerelease units	April 15 year 2
Preproduction run completed	February 15 year 2
Design and implement sales distribution and marketing strategy	November 15
	September 15 year 2
Prototype testing completed and approved	November 15
Align product and program capabilities with defined customer needs	October 15
Design and implement a certified supplier program	October 15
Get corporate approval for program to go ahead	September 15
Define budget requirements	August 15
Define product design and production requirements	July 15
Get corporate approval of the fully defined concept and technology	July 15
Implement a sign off system for ongoing program approvals	June 15
Define customer motivations and needs	June 15
Staff work centers with qualified people	ongoing

Current reality:

• 112 qualified developer capacity • financial resources available upon corporate
approvals • technology is proven but not fully defined • concept well defined
• some sub components are built & tested • corporate profit center not defined
• five large customers with signed contracts • twelve prospect customers
with good interest • supplier contacts in early development

Making Sure That Success Succeeds. Once this process is complete, we have defined the major goal(s) that express the business strategy; we have determined the current reality in relationship to our desired state; and we have defined the major actions that must be taken to accomplish our goal—*the management strategy.*

This is certainly helpful, but there is a danger here. People may begin to think that structural tension is merely a project management system, rather than *the* key structural mechanism that ties all parts of the organization together into a comprehensive whole. How can this be avoided? Do not simply organize actions to support an end result, but carefully place the actions in the context, not only of senior-level end results, but also in context of current realities *throughout the organization.*

Current reality changes as we do our work. Current reality is not the situation that existed the last time we happened to look. It needs continually to be updated. As we complete action steps, their accomplishments need to be listed. Situations we hadn't known about when we constructed our first structural tension chart must be added at each reality check and addressed forthwith. Perhaps we need to include new action steps to address these changes in reality. As we execute action plans, we make mistakes. How do we learn from those mistakes? How do we *incorporate* our learning? Some of this information will need to appear in updates of current reality and adjustments to our action plans.

Structural tension manifests itself most evidently throughout the organization in the conversations people have. Instead of What's the problem? How do we solve it?, we may hear people ask, What is the end result we are working on? *The end result is described* Where are we now?, *current reality is described and updated* What are we doing?, *the actions are described* How are they working?, *the actions are reviewed and evaluated* How should we proceed?, *plans are adjusted or changed based on the learning.*

Notice that, within this form, a sequence of hierarchical relationships is established, and success leads to success.

It is important that people use structural tension as the structure, and not a mindless mechanism. If we didn't have a structural tension charting process, we could still have structural tension as the dominant structure. In fact, many good managers unconsciously use a form of structural tension in their thought processes. One very effective plant manager of one of our client organizations had trouble understanding why his management group needed to write down the end result, the current reality, and the action steps.

"I always do that in my head," he said. "So why write it down?" "So other people will know what's in your head," one of his co-workers quickly chimed in, "and then we can help you for a change!"

As South Tech's managers went through the process of developing their first structural tension chart, they were discussing the relationship of certain steps to other steps. Some steps needed to be in place before related steps could be taken. Other steps were not as closely related. Of course, this first pass through the action planning stage was an overview approach. The details would be worked out later in using a technique called *telescoping*.

As South Tech's managers studied the twenty-six major actions they had established, they were able to see clearly for the first time what the successful completion of the project demanded.

They could see the relationship between technical demands and marketing demands. They could now envision just how the parts would fit together.

This master plan was the basis for South Tech's management strategy. All management activities were tied to their senior-level business strategy of *time to market*, and everyone understood the logic of the system.

This was only Phase One of South Tech's broader business strategy.

The Second-Phase Strategy

The longer-term strategy had to do with what South Tech wanted for itself—the *type* of business it wanted to be in longer term. South Tech did not want to build up a large tech-support division within the organization. While they needed one to support the first phase of the strategy, they wanted to phase it out over time by engineering more sophisticated technology into the product. Eventually they wanted to develop a stand-alone product that was so highly engineered that they could shrink wrap and ship it.

South Tech's Two-Phased Business Strategy

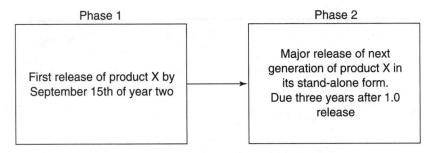

Phase 1	Phase 2
First release of product X by September 15th of year two	Major release of next generation of product X in its stand-alone form. Due three years after 1.0 release

South Tech thus created another, longer-term, structural tension chart with a desired end result of creating a product that could be packed and shipped. Then South Tech went through the same process as in Phase One to define the current reality and an action plan.

One other decision derived from the time-to-market strategy was how much tech support the first release would require. For South Tech to meet its timetable, it needed to build a tech-support capacity for Phase One of the strategy. Given the market's demand for acceptable quality, the first release had to work brilliantly. What South Tech couldn't design in at first would be provided by highly responsive tech support and special customer tailoring and adaptation. Over a three-year period after first release of the product, South Tech would design in more and more technology.

Simplicity and Complexity. As we review the chart that South Tech created, we might think it a simple to-do list. However, the structural tension chart does more than that. *It helps the organization structure events in time and put them in context with thematic unity.* In fact, when we begin to see the special way the master structural tension chart is developed and refined throughout the organization, we will begin to appreciate the simple elegance that becomes the basis for wonderfully structured complexity. Complexity as well structured as this is relatively easy to manage and reinforce. But the complexity rests on a foundation that can seem simple at first—that is simple at face value. However, once we begin to develop the next levels of detail, what seemed simple becomes expanded into a well-woven managerial counterpoint in which the parts fit together exquisitely.

Telescoping: Beyond Strategies

Each action step in the structural tension chart can be the basis for a new structural tension chart. This process is called *telescoping*.

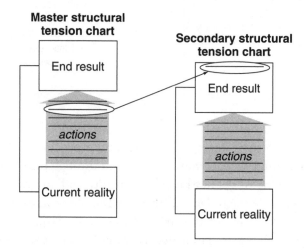

The organizing principle is to take a simple form—the structural tension form—and repeat the form in every managerial level throughout the organization. All actions will lead back to the master structural tension chart. All changes in current reality are tracked and recorded on the various structural tension charts, and are available to anyone in the entire management system who needs them.

Telescoping can be illustrated by using the third action steps from South Tech's master tension chart for the first-phase business strategy: Build the hardware/software by March 1 of year 2 (see the illustration at the top of the next page).

DESIRED END RESULT:
Prototype testing completed and approved by November 15

Actions	Completion/Due Date
Final changes to prototype completed and final test	November 07
Preliminary test of prototype	November 01
Complete preliminary supplier list	November 01
Identify sources for any new parts	October 15
Complete final drawings for prototype	October 15
Agree on changes based on preprototype testing	September 30
Complete field testing on preprototypes	August 15
Complete preprototype units based on product design	August 30
Prove out technology through field and lab testing	July 30
Preliminary drawings completed ready for corporate approval	July 07
Customer motivations and needs study adapted into design	June 30
Have qualified staff assigned to program	June 15

Current Reality as of May 15
• technology is proven but not fully defined • concept well defined • some sub components are built and tested • supplier contacts in early development • qualified staff available but not assigned to the program

---

This action step becomes the end result — the desired state. The current reality is then identified, and a new group of action steps are defined.

Each new structural tension chart can be the basis for other structural tension charts, until the entire project is planned and managed by the use of these charts:

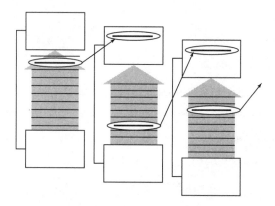

Telescoping reinforces structural tension as the dominant structure within an organization. It also develops hierarchical relationships and fuses them into an organizational structure that is a unified whole. As La France's George Barrar reported:

> These days we see interconnectedness throughout the business—how the different departments impact each other as part of our master design. We took our business strategy and then made strategic plans for each particular business unit across the corporation. When we put all the structural tension charts on the wall, it was really pretty obvious what the priorities were—where we needed to build up capacity, and where we needed to shift our focus, and where we didn't need to do what we thought we needed to do. It was pretty easy to make important decisions about direction and strategy, and now the organization is tremendously focused, and everything supports everything else.

In music, complexity is not only analyzed, it is also created. An organizational lesson can be learned by understanding how twentieth-century orchestral music, containing up to eighty-part counterpoint, is constructed and managed. This is how it is often done: Simple units of structure, called *cellular structures*, are placed into various instrumental parts. By using these repeatable devices, the handling of complexity becomes manageable; the result is that, while the orchestral texture can be complex, the music projects a very strong thematic unity. Igor Stravinsky, among others, was a master of this approach.

There is nothing as structurally complex in any organization as Stravinsky's *Rite of Spring* or *Firebird Suite*. However, because most people have had little training in or exposure to structure, they think organizations are difficult to organize. The only difficulty in bringing order to an organization is structural know-how, good structural design, and good management and leadership practices that will implement the structure. From a structural point of view, it is not the most difficult of tasks.

The principle of cellular unity is used when we take the master structural tension chart, and repeat the *form* in all the other dimensions of the organization. When we do that, complexity becomes manageable systemwide. The key is using the same form of structure from top to bottom of the organization.

There are enormous advantages to this structural approach. The business strategy is reinforced by the management strategy. The management strategy is reinforced by divisional or local strategies. Information can be tracked to update current reality systemwide, and overall adjustments in coordination can be well managed.

Besides the pure organizing advantages, this approach has other exceptional advantages. The thought process of an organization using this approach changes dramatically.

In the next chapter, we will look more closely at advantages and challenges of using a structural approach toward organizational development.

Quick Review

- The only way that organizations can really change is not by a change in behavior or process systems, but by a change in structure.

- The sixth law of organizational structure is: **If the organization's structure remains unchanged, the organization's behavior will revert back to the previous behavior.**

- The seventh law of organizational structure is: **A change in structure leads to a change of the organization's behavior.**

- Structural tension within an organization is hierarchical: The tension in the organization's purpose give direction to and is consistent with the business strategy, which in turn gives direction to and is consistent with the management strategy, and so on through the organization's other levels.

- The action plan consists of the steps needed to move the organization from its current reality to its desired state.

- A progression is the momentum that is created by a cycle in which action leads to results, which lead to evaluations, which lead to adjustments, which lead to new actions. This system develops increased capability over time.

- Telescoping reinforces structural tension throughout the organization by using each action in a structural tension chart as the basis for a new structural tension chart that reinforces the original chart.

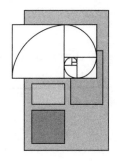

CHAPTER 10

The Structural Approach

This chapter expands the discussion about telescoping and uses several examples to demonstrate how structural tension charts achieve the organization's overriding strategy. There is a marked comparison between companies' operations before and after a structural approach was implemented. Improvement in productivity is easy to measure, and outcomes are readily seen after just a short period of time. Other benefits less directly measurable, but just as tangible, include the organization's ability to be in control of its direction, higher morale and involvement of its members, and faster, wiser business and management decisions.

The Use of Telescoping

When telescoping is used, each action step becomes its own structural tension chart. Within the organization using structural tension charting, the first phase therefore involves one (or sometimes two) major business strategy goals, supported by twenty to thirty other structural tension charts. These charts generate new action steps that become the basis for their own charts, and so on.

Often an organization will have from forty to over a hundred charts in operation. While this may sound like a fairly complex system, it is actually rather easy to manage, because each chart relates to another chart, and because most teams are managing only about ten charts or less.

Much of the work of these teams would have been done anyway, but in a less efficient and economic fashion. Using the charts to organize the workload greatly reduces managerial burden and strain.

A typical approach toward managing this process is found in the example of a pharmaceutical company's clinical research trial group. They were conducting a clinical study designed to test an anti-viral drug and—if it were found safe—bring it through the FDA regulatory process. The original structural tension chart was developed from the goal of receiving FDA approval; this was the desired state. Achieving this goal required a structural tension chart with twenty-three major action steps. Each step was then in turn developed into a structural tension chart. Finally, these twenty-three charts were telescoped into 144 charts. The charts represent the entire projects.

The senior manager of the group worked with her team by managing the master plan—the original structural tension chart. She also used her technical expertise to guide the process as difficulties and challenges arose, and to stay current with the very latest science concerning the disease related to their drug. The responsibility of each of the other charts was assigned to a person in one of the clinical teams, and two particular managers were assigned the task of coordinating the work flow.

These two managers set up what they called the war room, a room in which they could hang all of the structural tension charts around the walls. Anyone visiting that room could see the current state of the project in any of its phases. One of the two managers used traditional project management techniques in conjunction with the structural tension charts, working with members of the group to make sure that the trials were being carried out on time and within the correct protocol. Using each team's structural tension charts, the managers could easily track actions and update current reality as it changed. New steps were added as needed, and adjustments were continually made to support the time lines the group had created.

The other manager coordinated the flow and the relationships among the various charts so that, as the situation changed, an early warning system could alert the rest of the key players and they could replan as needed.

This was a good system: leadership management for the major structural tension chart, project management for the team work, and an overall manager who was coordinating and integrating the entire effort. Pharmaceutical development is especially relational, because every part is inextricably tied to the other parts. Information must be tracked and recorded precisely and the protocol must be adhered to with great discipline and rigor. Structural tension charting was particularly well suited to the demands of such a regimen.

Using Structural Tension Charts

Organizations that use a structural approach throughout their company find a new vitality and direction. They are able to accomplish real and lasting change as they move from structural oscillation to structural advancement. A different structure gives rise to a totally different experience within the organization. Not only can people become more productive, but they are also truly able to incorporate learning, innovation, and higher levels of professionalism into the team, the division, and the company as a whole.

Using Structural Tension Charts in a Manufacturing Company

In a conference on the structural approach in organizations, Gordon Baker, CEO for a mid-sized manufacturing company, and Rick Coulton, director of human resources, gave the following report about using a structural approach in their organization, a company with two divisions: the manufacture of high tech equipment that tests the hardness of various materials, and the manufacture and distribution of a plastic tubing.

Rick: In the past we had strategic business plans. Like most businesses do.

Gordon: Yeah, short-term, unconnected plans. More localized plans. Like most other businesses. We started building our strategic plan with structural tension charts and, after we had set them up, we had subsequent meetings to condense and rework them. We could really see the tension building. People were moving toward something that was meaningful to our business. Now we have comprehensive plans where everything fits together within the whole business.

Rick: We ended up with a really comprehensive business and management strategy. The two pivotal points of our business strategy translated into 22 major action steps.

Gordon: The beauty of this kind of well-designed structure is that nothing is arbitrary and people know that it's relevant—versus, we're doing a bunch of stuff and we don't know why we're doing it. Now, everything is driven by two key business strategies, from which we branched off management strategies. Subsequently, we ended up with local strategies coming off each one of those management strategies, which were really down at the level of getting the work done. So right now we're managing, I believe it's somewhere in the range of 40 structural tension charts that are linked back to these other management strategies, that are linked back to our business strategies. So everything is linked to everything else. No matter what you're working on, you know why you're doing it, all the way back up to our major business strategies.

Rick: There's a real clarity within the company now, because you're either working on one of two things: You're either doing core business strategy or you're working on growth strategy. Where before, with all the trainings, it was all "fluffy." You wondered What am I getting out of this?

Gordon: Core business is our day-to-day operations—processing orders, making stuff, getting it out. But people now really understand the relationship between the core business and our growth strategy.

Rick: And people are really working well together.

Gordon: Cooperation's much better . . .

Rick: And, where before, when we tried to get something done, people felt Well, hey, I've got other stuff I gotta work on. And you could never get things done right away. But now, people see what's needed and why, and they help get the job done.

Gordon: It's also easier to set up a hierarchy of what's to be worked on. However, we do have some bottlenecks—some limited resources in a given area. It's far easier to see what we need overall, and how we're going to (on a hierarchical basis) come up with decisions on what to work on first and what we can temporarily set aside.

Rick: Before, when we would change direction, it was "Ah, cripes, here we go again." But the other benefit is that now they know what's going on. "OK, if we need to move up this action step then, all right, let's put this other action step back here." And it's energetic, because everybody's aware of what we're trying to accomplish. They can see it. It's tangible.

Gordon: Exactly. They see why something's being set aside. Before, they didn't. Now, because the structure's in place, everyone knows exactly where and why changes fit in.

Rick: And we make decisions faster. We just had a case where we wanted to make a major decision about adding capacity.

Gordon: Right.

Rick: Now, normally, we would have gotten as far as saying We know we gotta do something here, but somehow it would never have gotten done. Now, within ten minutes, we made a decision. Everybody was in agreement with it, and we looked at each other thinking Who are these people? Twelve months ago that decision probably wouldn't have been made. We would have backed down. But now, when it was first brought up—Hey, I think we want to move this item up on our list—we were able to say Here's what's involved with this. So we're going to have to take a piece of this out. OK, move it up.

Gordon: It would have taken us an hour and a half to discuss it and nothing would have been decided; it would probably have *been put off for another meeting. Actually, meetings are almost non-existent now. In fact, we just huddle at the end of the week. Our management groups stand around structural tension charts and, basically, report in on what we're doing. If we've got to change some dates or change some priorities, at that time we decide what we're going to do, and we understand why we're going to do it.*

Rick: *Takes about a half hour.*

Gordon: *A half hour. That's another big change. Before, the management meetings went nowhere and they were taking up a lot of time. We were holding meetings every week whether we needed them or not. Sometimes the meetings were dragging into two and three hours. With not really much being accomplished. We were killing our own productivity by spending time in meaningless meetings.*

Now, I think our organization has more of the characteristics of an organization that is learning. We are definitely able to work more effectively as a team. I mean, you can actually see people working interdependently. Now they understand their relationship to one another—that they are interdependent. Everyone can see how it's working, why it's working. So by having—and working with—the structural tension charts, they feel better about what they are doing. They're proud of their accomplishments. Last year we were only at 17% growth, but we're on our target for a 25% increase this year.

Gary Ralston, a structural consultant and Principal of Catalytic Communications, Inc., Vancouver, Canada, reports on his use of structural tension charting:

One of our clients boiled a complex, urgent development project down to a master chart and fifteen sub-charts. By tacking them up on a wall and studying them all at once, she was able to discern key relationships between sub-tasks that had previously been hidden from view. She called in one of her colleagues, the person managing the technology developments of the project and, standing in front of the charts, reworked the approach they were taking. This change would never have happened if they were not able to see the entire project as parts related to the whole, something that would have been unlikely without the structural tension charting process. This insight led to design changes that shortened the development cycle, which was vital, given the company's deadlines.

Even teams operating within a large organization can use structural tension charting to accomplish projects more effectively and efficiently. Barry Sagotsky, an in-house training manager and structural consultant for Schering-Plough Pharmaceuticals, describes his use of structural tension charting with eighteen people from a health care systems group:

> They had to put together a white paper about whether or not to get into a particular business. Typically white papers in this organization take months to complete. We built the overall strategy for building a business at a certain volume over a five year period—a master structural tension chart and thirteen telescoped elements, each with their own structural tension charts. It was complete enough in the two days that we took to do the planning, that about 90 percent of the paper was completed. In two days! And this was a group that included three members who opened up their introduction of themselves by saying, "I don't think we can do this with this group, and I object to being here." At the end, the entire group had focused on making all thirteen steps in the structural tension charts happen.

Automating the Process

As we might imagine, these charts manage a lot of information. As action steps are carried out, reality changes. Current reality needs to be updated, adjustments need to be made, and people need to be made aware of critical changes that affect their management focus. To ease the facilitation of this process, we now use a special software program created by The Fritz Consulting Group in association with Choicepoint, Inc. The software, *Structural Tension Pro,* automates the *entire* process. While it can be done manually, this software aid is enormously helpful because it manages complex systems, alerts managers to changes in current reality, automates scheduling of events, and enables people to learn the system fast and effectively. While this is one of our products, and I am happy to recommend it for the most commercial of reasons, the deeper point here is central to the development and furtherance of using structural dynamics within an organization. Our system of computer automation is able to dramatically accelerate the process of bringing the best structural design into an organization, and it helps make the best use of the inescapable laws of organizational structure easily accessible. So, sorry for this sounding like a commercial, but the point is this: In the future, computer automation will make structural complexity within management systems easier and easier to handle.

Quick Review

- One master structural tension chart may be telescoped into a hundred or more supportive structural tension charts that guide the business and management activities of a well-structured organization.

- Companies that have used structural tension charts experienced a new and sustainable vitality. Extraneous discussions and meetings are reduced because energies are focused on what needs to be accomplished within the structural tension charts.

- A software program, *Structural Tension Pro,* is available through Choicepoint, Inc. It automates the entire process, providing a means to manage, update, communicate, and distribute information, and to coordinate all the activities of all the structural tension charts.

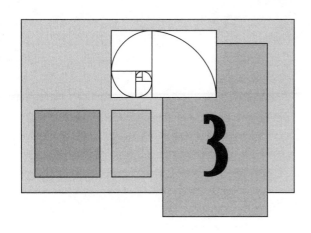

Structural
Thinking

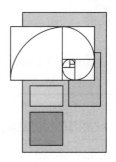

CHAPTER 11

Frames
How We See Reality

Part 2 of this book discussed how to identify the current reality and the desired state and how to use the tension between them to advance the organization. Because one of the two elements in this structure is the current state, essential to this process is an objective perception of reality. Part 3 will focus on how we think, and how we can develop the process of structural thinking to better understand current reality objectively and accurately. One crucial aspect of structural thinking is to become fluent in current reality—in viewing reality objectively. There are many built-in impediments to seeing reality objectively, which we will address, but there is one impediment that stands above all the rest, and that is the *usual* way we think. In fact, as we will see, we have not been taught to think. Instead we have been taught to use information as a "data base," and then compare reality with what we already know.

Structural thinking is a skill that can be learned and developed, but not by the usual ways we have been trained to think, so Part 3 will introduce you to new ways to use your mind. This chapter begins this process by examining how we frame our thinking toward the world around us. Understanding how we see these dimensions will enable us to understand how we view reality, and what frame of reference is optimal for our purposes.

Framing Reality

When people use structural tension charting, one of the important challenges is that they must think differently. The change is from thinking linearly in small units to thinking dimensionally in larger units.

What is the framework by which we look at reality? Imagine we had a video camera. We could shoot a close-up, a medium shot, or a long shot. When we play the video on a television monitor, the size of the picture would be the same: 13 inches, or 17, or 21 inches or whatever the monitor's size; whatever type of shot we made, it would fill the entire screen (see illustration). Each type of shot is a particular frame of reference.

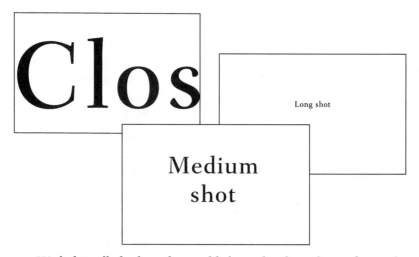

We habitually look at the world through a lens that is focused on a close-up, a medium shot, or a long shot. We can move from one type of shot to another, but usually we don't.

A structural approach requires a fluency in current reality. To become fluent, we may need to learn how to observe, process information, and make critical distinctions in new ways. We need to be able to change our frame of reference easily. Let's explore each of these three frames of reference and how to change from one to another.

The Close-Up: Immediate Events and Obsessive Detail

Some people use the close-up as their primary frame of reference, focusing on the immediate events that confront them. They tend to obsess about details but can often miss what the various details, put together, imply.

Organizations are filled with people who use immediate events and obsessive detail as their frame of reference. We can see this trait by how they relate to time. Time, to these people, comes in short phases. If a conversation is going on about the budget over the next three years, or a product development strategy for a ten-year period, this person will talk about the company's immediate problems. They might pick out a detail from the general overview, and focus their attention on it. They think they are adding a missing piece; the devil is in the details, and they are playing a form of devil's advocate.

When managers who are assigned the overall leadership of a project, or department, or division think in this close-up frame of reference, they can easily be overwhelmed. It's because of the way they take in information, bit by bit. It is hard to hold on to so high a volume of bits, and eventually they run out of the mental capacity to do so.

Such people would see the world as complicated and hard to manage. They might have high aspirations and deeply held values, but their way of relating to information greatly limits their effectiveness. In spite of their aspirations, they would be forced to react or respond to the immediate circumstances in which they find themselves. The experience would be that of treading water.

However, even if you have had your lens zoomed in on a close-up your whole life, you can zoom back. You can change your frame.

The Long Shot: Chronic Vagueness

If we back up too far, we can no longer make out what is before us. Some people habitually look at the world through a lens that is so wide that everything seems to fuse together in an indistinguishable haze. They know that something is there, but they can't quite make out what it is. These people think in very long time periods, and they often ponder the distant future more than the current reality.

These days, this frame of reference is more prevalent within organizations than we might imagine, and it takes the form of chronic vagueness. Phrases such as "customer-focused" or "increased sales" or "quality" or "organizational learning" can give the impression that something important is being said. But just what? When something remains that vague, it seems remote, an abstract idea and not a reality.

People who live in the long shot quite often speculate about how the world is because, without a clear view of current reality, it gives them a way to get their bearings. Managers who are vague often attempt to be inspirational because, if they are to mobilize the people who they manage, they cannot rely on a concrete world they have trouble seeing.

Instead, such a manager will use the feeling tone of the group to determine progress. If the members fall from grace of the inspirational atmosphere, speeches are given, hands are held, and warm feelings are projected. Whether or not the feeling tone is restored, the chronic vagueness makes it hard for these managers to move forward toward desired results.

Even managers who think they use a systems approach in their work sometimes are not thinking systemically at all, but merely presuming some kind of "everything is connected and we are all one" world view. To truly think systemically, one must see exactly how elements are connected and what types of relationships they form. One must discern the system *in fact*, rather than simply impose a general systems notion on reality.

Since structural tension is formed by the discrepancy between the desired end state and current reality, if reality is missing, all the vision in the world will not help and the organization will slip into structural oscillation.

If you have a long-shot frame of reference, you can change. Qualities such as love, loyalty, selflessness and professionalism can be real but, for us to see them, they need to be translated into action. As in the world of theater and films, character is action. We know Hamlet by virtue of the actions he takes in confronting the conflict of loyalties between supporting his mother's happiness and finding justice for his dead father's ghost. Hamlet's character is seen by his *actions*, not what he says about his actions. The same is true in "non-fictional" life. Warm-sounding concepts are meaningless until they are supported by actions; then they can be easily seen. We have moved from the haze of vagueness to the clarity of shape; we have changed focus from the long shot to the medium shot.

Some organizations have both a high concentration of obsessively detailed people who are driven by immediate events and a high number of people who are chronically vague. This is not a winning combination. Within these organizations we seem to have a choice between extremes. We can sloganeer with the company's "visionaries," or we can plow through tons of information that simply overwhelms us. Conflicts within these organizations seem unaddressable. There is no meeting of the minds, for the two different types are speaking an entirely different language. But, because both of these frames of reference are ineffective, no one group ever dominates. When organizations like this attempt to become a "learning organization," some will use the opportunity to preach their various world views while others will attempt to tutor people in how to deal with the minutiae.

The Medium Shot: Objective Shapes, Trends, and Patterns

The medium shot enables us to observe both the forest *and* the trees. We can make out details, but we can also recognize the relationships formed by these details. As we back away from a close-up, or move in from a long shot, we reach a point where we can see shapes and patterns. We can see the shapes just as clearly as we see various objects. By observing from some degree of distance or separation, we can perceive reality[1] with a perspective that leads to understanding the spatial relationships various objects have with each other.

With a medium-shot frame, time is observed very differently than it is from the other two frames. We can observe the present, but also how the present connects with the past and how the present may play itself out in the future. If a baseball player hit a ball toward center field, and the ball was high in the air and moving out fast, we would be able to predict to some degree where it is likely to land. This is why sports announcers can watch a solidly hit baseball sail out toward the fence and say "Going! Going! Gone!" If they couldn't predict

---

[1]The term *reality* here is not ultimate reality or absolute truth. It is not *Reality* with a capital R. The term is used to describe our normal, everyday reality where there are numbers, people, movement, and so on. To understand this use of the term, do not apply philosophical or metaphysical standards.

where the ball might land, they would have to say "Don't know, don't know . . . oh, wow, it suddenly went over the wall!"

The values in using a medium-shot frame of reference is that we are able to get more useable information than we could otherwise. Both the close-up and the long shot give us information, but they are like *non*-relational databases; the information base cannot connect with various other bases. But the medium shot—the objective vantage point of shape and pattern—is like a relational database in which things that do in fact connect, can be seen as connecting.

Of course, seeing patterns and trends provides us with insight about cause and effect, and the consequences of the actions we have taken, are taking, or might take in the future. When we study reality on this level, we can evaluate ourselves. Were our impressions accurate? Were we able to take action at the most opportune time because we understood how the patterns would play themselves out over time?

We can see the shapes and patterns that reality forms, when we are able to move in at will for a close-up if we need more detail. When we need a broader perspective, we can back up for a long shot. In either case we are able to take in information and relate it to its proper context. We can delve into relevant details but not obsess about them. We can observe reality from a great panorama but not get lost in abstruseness. We can observe reality objectively.

Thinking Dimensionally

When organizations begin to use the structural approach, one of the important changes that takes form is how the members of the organization relate to time. Time begins to move dimensionally rather than linearly. People do think in linear time frames; there are due dates and start dates. They are not simply slaves to a ticking clock, but understand how *events take shape in time*. Time does not move in only one dimension. We experience a "counterpoint" of different time zones that occur simultaneously. We meet a friend we haven't seen for years, and suddenly all the intervening years can seem compressed. In the waiting room of our dentist, ten minutes can seem like three hours.

When an organization uses the structural approach, various time frames fit together. Short-term results fit together with long-term results. We are able to see the shapes and patterns of time, events, and various networks of relationships.

The organization learns how to think of time from the broad perspective of the purpose and business strategy and, simultaneously, the shorter levels of the management and local strategies. As we monitor changes in current reality, information can be tracked through one level of structural tension charting, and transform itself to fit the next higher level. We can move in when we have to, and back up when we have to. We can have conversations with each other that are in the same language.

Choosing the optimal frame of reference is only one step in seeing reality objectively. We shall explore the next steps in the following chapter.

Quick Review

- A structural approach requires dimensional thinking—thinking in multiple units—rather than the usual linear thinking.

- Thinking can be done from a close-, medium- or long-shot frame of reference.

- A close-up shot is focused on immediate events and excessive details. People who use this frame of reference are often so filled with concern about details that they can miss what the details mean in relation to each other. They can miss the forest because they are so focused on the trees.

- A long shot is vague and ill defined. People who use this frame of reference often substitute platitudes for clear observations about reality.

- A medium shot is the preferred frame of reference because objective shapes, trends, and patterns in reality can be best understood; details can be understood in context, and the more meaningful details can be better explored.

- It is possible to change frames as a first step in learning how to think structurally.

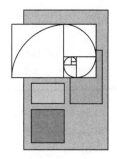

CHAPTER 12

Thinking Structurally

For over fifteen years the area of objective thinking, and particularly *structural* thinking, has been critical to my work. This body of work in structural thinking first evolved when I began training instructors in my methods. We found that most people could not learn to use a structural approach until they changed the way they thought. Not *what* they thought, not the content of their ideas, beliefs, opinions, experiences, or theories, but how they observed reality and processed information. *How* they thought.

This chapter introduces you to the methodology called structural thinking, which is an invaluable skill in discerning reality both astutely and quickly. Since the foundation for structural tension is current reality, managers and organizations must be able to move from subjective "impressionistic" interpretation about reality to objective "photorealistic" observation. Consequently, before we discuss objective observation and structural thinking, we must explore how people usually think.

If we wanted to travel to San Francisco, but we didn't know our current location, how could we get there? We would find it very hard indeed. Without a fix on reality, we wouldn't know our current location in relationship to our desired location, and what actions to take that would bring us to our desired location.

Observing reality objectively is extremely important in the life of an organization, for without knowing what exists *in reality*, structural tension cannot be created and structural oscillation will dominate the company.

When we begin to talk about reality, some people are prone to say, "whose reality?" Their idea is that we cannot say anything meaningful about *objective* reality, because to them reality is completely subject to interpretation. To them, objective reality doesn't exist.

Sometimes they also think that how one views reality changes it —that reality is influenced by our thoughts about it.

This is a fairly philosophical point of view, and they might be right in some Ultimate sense. But this point of view is hardly ever at issue when these very same people ask their accountants to do their tax returns. To the tax man, the accountant, *and* the accountant's client, the numbers are the numbers, and they don't change no matter how a person thinks about them. We could say that objective reality exists in the same domain as do numbers, tax returns, and the people who use them.

Objective reality here is not a philosophical concept; it is not in the domain of Absolute Truth. It is simply a way to observe what exists in what we might call "local reality," the reality in which objects seem to move in time and space.

Here's the question we need to confront: Is reality the way it is *because* we observe it (subjective), or is reality the way it is *whether or not* we observe it (objective)?

If a tree falls in the forest, but no one is there to witness it fall, does it really fall? Does reality exist because we know it to exist, or does it exist independent of our perceptions? And why, when we come later, do we find a fallen tree on the ground?

In structural thinking, when it comes to current reality in relationship to a desired result, reality exists *independent from* our perceptions. How do we know that? Because if we are not accurate about current reality we weaken structural tension, we are less able to adjust our actions effectively, and *tangible* unwanted consequences will result; if we think we're in Phoenix but we're really in Nashville, getting to San Francisco will be very difficult. When we become more accurate, structural tension is stronger and there is more energy and power to motivate our actions. We can adjust our actions more astutely; our ability to create our desired results is improved greatly.

One essential learning that benefits organizations enormously is how to think objectively. How to think objectively is a prerequisite for thinking structurally.

Comparative Thinking

All of us have been taught to think comparatively. We acquire facts, theories, experiences, and information. What do we do with what we accumulate? When we look at reality, we compare what we see with our preexisting personal database.

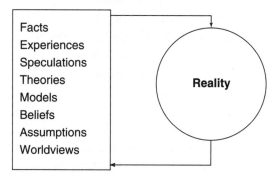

We look for a match. If we see something that looks like something we have experienced or known in the past, we categorize it. Why do we do that? Because we want to make order of the world. Confronted by the unknown or incomprehensible, we would experience a strong sense of disorder.

We not only identify specific elements and then categorize them based on our personal database, we also place each item into a *context*—a relationship with other items. We want everything to fit. We crave an orderly world and universe.

We look at the world with a notion of how it will be, how it works, what we might find, how to relate to what we might encounter—and we are hardly ever surprised, because the world seems to conform to our expectations. This is why we know we are right. Our expectations about the world, *whatever they are*, will almost always prove themselves to be correct.

When they prove themselves to be incorrect, we have one of two choices. We can deny reality, or we can form a new context that accommodates the new data. One way or another, we will have restored a sense of order in the world, for *the goal of a comparative thought process is not truth but order*.

Seeing What We Expect to See

Comparative thinking is a "this reminds me of that" process. When something new comes into our awareness, something we have not encountered in the past, something for which we have no frame of comparison, we invent a context. We usually speculate and theorize. What is the function of speculation and theory? To give us the impression that we know *more* than we actually know. To connect facts that do not yet have an apparent connection.

We use our assumptions as a convenience. When we assume something to be true, we don't need to find out if it is indeed true. We have developed a habit of *assuming* what reality is, rather than *looking* at how it actually is. Even when we think we are looking, we are not always seeing what is there. And often we see something that isn't really there at all.

Arthur Stern, a wonderful artist and teacher, makes this point in his book *Color—How to See and Paint It*: "Many painters don't paint what they see, but what they expect to see, what they think they see, what they remember, or what they imagine things are supposed to look like."

Stern tells the story of taking a group of his students to Riverside Park to look across the Hudson at New Jersey. He pointed to three architectural structures: an apartment house at the top of the Palisades; a storage tank down at the waterside; and a tall factory further up the river. He then asked "What color are those buildings?"

His students all gave him the same answers. The apartments were red. ("Red brick," someone said.) The storage tanks were white. And the factory was orange.

But then Stern handed around some small cards, each with a hole punched through it. He calls them spot screens. When people look through these cards at the objects in question, the color can be isolated, and seen out of context of the objects themselves. Once his students had the cards, he asked them to look through the hole.

"Now tell me what colors you see," Stern instructed his students. They became silent until finally one of them spoke up. "They're all blue, like the rest of the scenery over there when you look through the hole in the card." The other students joined in agreement. The red apartment house, the white tank, and the orange factory building all looked *blue*.

On hazy days, when we look off at the distant mountains, or across a river, or even down a long street, there is atmosphere between us and the distant objects. The atmosphere reflects light, often the light of the sky. That's why faraway mountains can look purple or blue. When the students isolated the color from the context of the buildings in question, they were forced to see what was *really* there. And they easily saw it, because it was there to see in objective reality.

In fact, it was always there to see, but they simply did not see what was before their eyes. Why not? Because they had a concept of what colors they thought they should see. They compared reality— the various buildings as they actually looked—to their notion of how these buildings should look. They ignored the information that didn't fit in with their notions. They happened to share the same concepts, so it was easy for them to agree about red, white, and orange.

Is this a trick of the mind, or is it that the mind works perfectly well for what it does, but we don't always happen to give it accurate information? In the Stern example, he knew his students were capable of seeing the actual color they were observing. That is why he brought the spot screen cards with him as part of his teaching approach. And, in fact, once they looked more precisely, the students could see what was there to see. But we must take a lesson from how they thought before they were given the cards.

People often substitute a concept of reality for reality. They then impose their concept on themselves. Since this is such a common thought process, some people think it is the *only* thought process. If they want to change people then they are left with only one option: to change people's basis of comparison—their assumptions, beliefs, opinions, and world views. People who hold this view are big on conversion. They think it is desperately important that people believe the "correct" thing, because if they don't they will use the wrong mental model in seeing the world and then (unfortunately) act accordingly.

It is not wrong or bad to hold opinions, or to have beliefs, or to think that the world or the universe is a particular way. But we must remember that when we make these factors a basis of comparison, we are imposing a *concept* of reality on the world.

There is a story of a man who was catching mice. One night he ran out of cheese for his mouse trap. So he left a picture of a big piece of cheese in the trap. In the morning he found he had caught a picture of a mouse.

A picture of a mouse is not a mouse, and a concept of reality is not reality.

REALITY: TRUTH AND ORDER

I suppose we must make a quick point about the reality we are talking about, because some people get a bit riled when it seems as if reality is being spoken of in concrete terms.

As we said before, the reality we are referring to here is not meant to be Absolute Truth, the ultimate reality. Instead, we could say that it is temporary "truth," that is, how reality *seems* to be on this plane in which there *seem* to be objects in space and time.

Concerning Absolute Truth: Perhaps in the end, beyond our life, what we think is reality may turn out to be an illusion. Perhaps it won't. But no matter what the Absolute truth is, does *speculating* about it give us real understanding? If we knew how Absolute reality *truly* was, would we need to rely on beliefs, theories, speculations, convictions, and so on?

No matter what we can say about reality, the true mysteries remain mysteries (for example, what is the universe and where is it?).

While we might feel better once science proclaims that the universe began with a big bang, we are still left with a mystery. Before the big bang, this big, big, big thing was hanging around somewhere. It exploded, and from that explosion all the stars and planets were created. What was there before this big thing? How did it get there? If the universe is expanding, as some scientists tell us, into *what* is it expanding? What's beyond the universe?

These questions are important to us because, when we are confronted with the unknown, we experience a state of disorder which we don't like. If we think we have found a plausible explanation, we have the impression of increased order. Many people are glad that science has finally verified the big bang theory, because it seems to give us the image of universal rhyme and reason. And we like that, because we like order.

This is why unifying theories about the universe are so popular. They give us a plausible explanation that ties everything together into a comprehensive whole. While we know as little now as we ever did concerning Absolute Truth, our impression is that we have made progress. However, if we were truly honest, we would be forced to admit that the true mysteries remain mysteries. Are we searching for *truth* or *order* when we pretend we know what we don't know?

Objective Reality

Training in both the visual arts and music brings students through rigorous drills that teach them to look and listen more precisely and objectively. Some of the exercises might involve taking a picture of a person, and turning it upside down.[1] When students know it's a face they often draw their concept of a face so, by turning the picture upside down, students are forced to look at it deliberately. This process enables them to render the likeness accurately.

In conservatories of music, students are taught ear training. Over many years, students learn how to identify accurately what they are hearing. In the more advanced stages of ear development, the student is able to listen to a recording of a symphony, and write down the entire score[2]. Students are graded on the accuracy of their work. If they write down accurately what was performed, they get an A. On this level, reality certainly is objectively observable. We can determine without question if the student's perception was accurate.

The world of accounting is another perfect example of this principle of objectivity. We would not want an accountant who used comparative thinking in his or her work:

"You know, I've seen many tax returns that look something like yours. In fact, I did one just last week. Now, in that case, the fellow paid $326.43 to the government. Tell you what, why don't you just send in that amount, and I'm sure it will be fine."

When you think comparatively in the world of accounting, you end up in jail.

---

[1] This is not to teach the brain to use the right hemisphere as has been reported, but to make the student scrutinize what is observed more consciously.

[2] In music schools, this is called a *record copy*.

The Nature of Language

Some people think the nature of language forces on us a built-in bias, impeding an objective view of reality. They are concerned that the structure of language influences our impressions and perhaps, even determines our impressions. This was a view I held for many years when, after studying music in Germany, I concluded that the difference between the structure of the German language and the English language led to very different possibilities of thought (of what *could* be thought). In those days I was concerned with the placement of verbs in the sentence, and how many distinctions the language had for the same object. Is there a word for love, or sadness, or truth, or death, or heaven, or hell?

I have changed my mind almost completely, because over the years, as I studied the structural make-up of various societies speaking different languages in different cultures, I was amazed at their commonalties, not the differences. Cultural differences certainly exist. But when it comes to why people behave as they do these differences were truly irrelevant. People's lives are filled with structural forces that give rise to consistent patterns of behavior, no matter what the cultural predisposition. Even if a culture and language does not have the word or concept of love, people still fall in love with each other and love their children. If they do not have a word for fear, they still experience anxiety when their child is in harm's way or a hurricane sweeps over the land.

In my view, language is not generative in that it does not *cause* reality to be any particular way. I agree with Shakespeare's observation that a rose by any other name would smell as sweet. It's not what you call a thing, it's what it is. And what it is isn't changed by what you call it. I also agree with Gertrude Stein, who observed "A rose is a rose is a rose." Isn't it, though?

We are not invented by language, but we use language to invent. If we don't have a word we need, we make one up. It is a matter of functionality of language: looking for the right word to say what we thought, rather than thinking because we have certain words available. This is why, with the coming of new technology, new words are being invented. By itself, language does not impede an objective view of reality. But what about the way we use language?

Let's look at how we use words.

Classification

Words set up categories of things. This is called a *class type*. A word becomes a way of grouping things of the same kind.

We use a comparative process in describing the world, but this process is not the same as comparative thinking in that it does not impose on reality a previous experience, opinion, belief, or theory. Instead, it simply identifies items that are members of a group, by naming them. These names can be used to describe individual objects or elements in relationship to other elements. By having these various names available to us we can easily identify elements and, having done that, form (or recognize) relationships among the various elements. This process is essential as we negotiate the world.

Similarities and Differences

We are able to identify specific objects by comparing their similarities and differences with corresponding objects in their class types.

If we see a cat, we do not need to rediscover what *cat* is. We observe qualities that are *common* to the group, but *different* for a specific individual. While we recognize a particular cat is *similar* to all other cats, we also identify the *unique* aspects of that particular cat.

We can also put similar attributes into different categories when necessary. A very large cat may be a mountain lion. The mountain lion shares many characteristics with the house cat, but the differences tell us that this beast is not Tabby and may not treat us with the same degree of affection.

The nature of language is *distinction*. When certain distinctions are made, the relationships between and among elements become easier to understand and manage.

Some people adopt a viewpoint that everything in the world is so connected that individual elements become indistinguishable from one another—a cat becomes indistinguishable from a mountain lion. The major deficit in this approach is that relationships are not well understood, because the constituent elements of the relationship are not clearly defined. To *presume* relationship is not the same as observing true relationships among elements. In the first case one understands very little, because the actual nature of any specific relationship remains stereotyped—an amorphous notion of conceptual connectedness. Those who hold this sentiment are considering *a picture of a relationship, not a real relationship*.

When we make clear distinctions, we are able to study the actual relationship that exists between and among elements. This ability enables us to see structural relationships as well as other types of relationships.

Observing Objectively

If we presume anything before we observe, we are less likely to see what is there to see, because we will tend to impose our concept of reality on what we are seeing. To form an opinion before we make observations results in biased or prejudicial thinking. To observe first, and then from that observation form opinions, is objective.

The term objective refers to an object. Reality as an *object* implies the basis of objective thinking. The implication is that we are separate from the rest of reality, and that reality can be observed just as we observe an object. This is a purely functional approach that allows us to better observe reality. In no way is it an attempt to create any form of self-definition. In this regard, self-definition is irrelevant.

We can take some objects in our hands and look at them—a piece of pottery, for example. We gaze at it, feeling its textures and weight. We may trace the shape of it with a finger. We can feel the temperature. We could smell the clay or enamel. We may study the design, the shape, the decoration, the colors. We may have opinions and visceral responses to the object. Some of these responses may be subjective, *but these subjective responses are produced by objective means*.

In the arts, objective means are used to create subjective effects. Alfred Hitchcock, a good example of the principle, would work diligently at structuring an entire film so that the emotional impact was predictable at every moment of the film. Through objective means he could determine what people would experience subjectively, and exactly when they would experience it.

We can place a piece of pottery on a table, walk away from it, and then view it from a greater distance. We can move around it and see it from various angles. We do not become fixed in our method of perception, or in our vantage point. Reality as an object provides some of the same advantages. Since we are not attempting to find Absolute Truth, we can see reality for what it is in our "local plane," objects in space in time in relationship to each other.

Without the ability to observe the actual elements that exist in objective reality, thinking structurally or systemically would be impossible, because we would not be able to understand the nature of the relationships formed by these elements. Thinking objectively is the first step in understanding the actual relationships that exist.

THINKING

Thinking is more than simply perceiving reality and then comparing our observations to our personal database of experiences, beliefs and concepts. And it is more than merely categorizing. To think is to **observe, separate, fuse,** and **assemble.** It's also to:

- **Generalize**—to form generic shapes from singular events or patterns

- **Individualize**—to establish a distinct classification for each new phenomenon

- **Systematize**—to create a sequence of levels, degrees, or steps

- **Conceive**—to imagine, suppose, visualize

- **Extrapolate**—to extend the direction of tendencies, so we can envision various outcomes based on past sequences or patterns.

- **Contrast**—to form differences

Most importantly, thinking is the ability to construct **relationships** among the various elements that are being considered and, then, to generate new sets of relationships.

These relationships give us an impression of understanding and a sense of orientation. We are able to know what the elements of a situation are, how they function, and how they impact each other.

Structural Thinking

When we think structurally, not only are we observing individual elements, events, and patterns, but we are also exploring sets of relationships that give rise to tendencies for behavior inherent to those relationships. We can understand that a predictable pattern of oscillation or advancement is taking place, and we are able to perceive the structural conflicts or tensions that cause it.

Furthermore, this knowledge enables us to restructure the forces in play to produce the behavior we desire, just as when we are restructuring a structural conflict into structural tension.

Our organizations and lives are products of countless structural interactions that are often invisible until we search them out. But they cannot be found when we do not know how to look.

Learning to Think in Structures

The following method is a thinking process that I originally developed to train instructors and consultants in our work. Over the years, we have developed quite a rigorous approach that brings people through an intellectually demanding method in thinking skills, structural analysis, organizational structure, and more. Those who demonstrate a firm grasp of the skill can become *Certified Structural Consultants*. People certified as structural consultants have demonstrated the ability to understand the forces in play in any situation they encounter, and they can then help people take strategic action designed to create desired outcomes.

Many managers, particularly those concerned with organizational leadership or organizational change, study structural thinking and consulting so they can rethink and redesign their organizations. The training enables these managers to be astute about the forces in play within their own organizations and industries.

Huib Bruijstens, a Philips Electronics NV program manager for technology management training, and an internal structural consultant, has said:

> Structural consulting makes it possible for my clients and me to see whether a request for a certain training program has any chance of bringing about the results the manager wants.

Structural consulting makes us understand, in a very efficient way, the forces in play that lead to the present behavior. Especially the representation of a structural conflict, if present, gives a deep and clear understanding about what's going on. This leads to discussions on the design of a suitable structure and quite often we conclude that this does not include a training program.

Often reality is obscured by faulty information and inaccurate assumptions. When the structural consultant and client co-explore objective reality, the client is then able to come to some essential insights about current reality that would not have been apparent through other means. In a recent seminar on organizational structural consulting, one of the guest clients was vice president of a major insurance company. Various structural consultants took turns working with this man in a demonstration in front of the group. The vice president made this observation about the structural consulting process:

> I've been struggling with the strategy issue for over a year. In less than two hours, the consultants understood our market and organization well enough to design a terrific business strategy. Most consultants ask for piles of information and details. That didn't happen here. The structural consultants only asked for the information they needed, and we came up with a great strategy. They really understood our business.

Tom Quimby, a mediator and structural consultant, uses structural consulting extensively in his work on labor–management issues, and also as an organizational consultant. He has found that a structural thinking approach allows him to penetrate the real issues people face as he helps them redesign their structure. He has seen people's chances of success increase greatly:

> Recently I was asked to work with an organization which was considering getting rid of, or transferring, a manager. The organization had recently had a change in leadership and the new CEO was much more concerned with people working together as a team. In an attempt to keep the manager where he was, and retain the benefit of his experience, they asked us to come in and work with him. At first, when we began working with the manager, he was hurt and understandably bitter. Using a structural approach, we helped him to identify what it really was he wanted to do and how that squared with current reality. We

considered the inevitable outcomes of his current way of relating to people, given the new changes in reality. We then worked on developing a new personal structural tension system which serves both him and the organization. This is working. He is happier because he really understands what's going on. He can now make real choices based on what he really wants rather than based on fear. It has systematized our whole approach and shifted the focus from blame to outcomes. It's great.

There are four distinct stages that occur organically when one is thinking structurally. They are:

Phase I—Observation

Phase II—Studying the relationships formed by the observed elements

Phase III—Structural analysis and conclusions

Phase IV—Working with the structure to redesign as needed

Phase I: Observation. This skill is developed by learning how to look at reality without a preconceived bias or basis for comparison. Most consulting and thinking methods begin with a model, theory, or set of experiences that is used to diagnose conditions. Once the client's conditions are categorized, prescriptions for changes are proposed. Although the nature of theories or experiences may vary widely from consultant to consultant and from method to method, the form of thinking is the identical—it is comparative. Managers use the same comparative thought process in their work, which often limits their ability to see and understand causal, structural relationships.

Structural thinking begins with nothing—without a frame of reference, a bias, or a predisposition.

Even the models of structural tension and structural conflict are better discovered by observing reality than by imposing them on reality. If these relationships actually exist, they will become obvious. If they do not, there is no need to pretend they do.

Phase II: Studying the Relationships Formed by the Observed Elements. Once we can understand the elements clearly, we can begin to examine the ways they influence each other, how they form shapes and patterns, and how they create tendencies for movement and behavior. Tension-resolution systems become obvious. Structural relationships can be studied and tested. Do they lead to predictable outcomes? Have they in the past? Can we observe patterns that advance or oscillate? We move back and forth between phase I and phase II, testing our perception of relationships against reality.

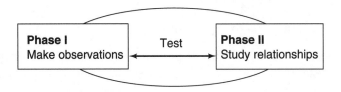

Phase III: Structural Analysis and Conclusions. After a period of testing the relationships against reality and continually correcting our impressions, we have ample evidence to make a conclusion about the nature of the structure. Then we will be able to predict the structure's behavior, and we can report accurately on what it has done. We know if we have the structure of a rocking chair or a car and we know how this structure will tend to behave.

Phase IV: Working with the Structure to Redesign as Needed. Because we understand the structure that is in place, we can work with it. We can consider our aspirations in relationship to the forces in play in reality, and design new and ever more functional structures for our purpose.

Additive Picturing

To help people learn structural thinking, I have developed a technique called *additive picturing*. Through it, we are translating information received into a visual language, and then adding each additional picture to previous pictures. At first the pictures might seem like a montage of loosely related (or even unrelated) images. Soon, however, internal commonalities and differences begin to appear. When we perceive information visually, relationships between elements often become obvious to us. Structures begin to appear, and causal relationships often become apparent. Additive picturing involves six steps:

1. Start with nothing.

2. Listen to what is being said.

3. Form pictures of the information.

4. Add each new picture to the other pictures.

5. Identify discrepancies.

6. Ask questions to explain discrepancies.

Start with Nothing.   This is probably the most difficult step for most people when they are first learning this skill. Is it possible to view reality without a past frame of reference? Yes. If we were accountants, no amount of previous experience would permit us to bypass observing the actual numbers.

The skill of starting a thought process without preconceptions or biases can be developed with practice. We can avoid our tendency to jump to association when we limit our frame of reference to our observations, and only our observations. Part of the discipline of this approach is that the consultant never presumes information that has not been observed.

Listen to What Is Being Said.   The client describes the current situation.

Form Pictures of the Information.   Perhaps the client says "I climbed a tree Saturday morning at 9:30." We form a picture of that person climbing a tree. Information that is not translatable into pictorial form needs better definition, so we ask questions until we can form a picture of it.

Add Each New Picture to the Other Pictures.   At first, the pictures may seem simply to be unrelated information. As we get more information, the pictures begin to form groupings. Clusters of relationships may then appear, and eventually deeper structural relationships emerge.

Identify Discrepancies.   As we listen, then form and add pictures, we will begin to observe discrepancies between two or more pictures.

For example, perhaps the client who said "I climbed a tree Saturday morning at 9:30" later tells us "I went home Saturday morning at 9:30." We have a picture of the client climbing a tree and going home in the same time period. This forms an apparent discrepancy.

Ask Questions to Explain Discrepancies.   There are only two possibilities when sorting out discrepancies. Either one or both of the points of information is inaccurate, or there is missing information that explains the apparent discrepancy.

Too often, when we are faced with discrepancy we tend to invent an explanation because we do not feel comfortable with dissonance. Also if the habit of jumping to associations is ingrained in us, we may not know that we have added our own explanation. By filling in our concept of what *might* have happened, we presume knowledge we don't actually have. The discrepancy will then become more obscure, and we will have the impression that we understand more than we do. Let's use the example of our tree-climbing chart to illustrate how to avoid this pitfall.

Did the person climb the tree or go home? There are a limited number of possibilities:

1. **One statement is true; the other isn't.** The statement "I climbed a tree Saturday morning at 9:30" may be true, and the other statement, "I went home on Saturday morning at 9:30" may be untrue, or vice versa. Or both may be inaccurate. We can ask questions that are focused toward explaining the discrepancy. The answers can point to which statement is accurate and which is not. Rather than an adversarial, police type of investigation, the consultant and client work together. How are we to explain this discrepancy?

2. **There is missing information that explains the discrepancy.** The other possibility is that both statements are true but there is information that we need to explain the apparent discrepancy. "I climbed a tree and went home on Saturday morning at 9:30 because I live in a tree house." The new information (home is in a tree) explains the situation, which no longer contains a discrepancy.

In a long conversation about complicated organizational issues many discrepancies will emerge. Often they are lost by a shorthand comparative thought process, and much valuable information is overlooked because of the bad habit of using speculation and conjecture to explain away discrepancies. This practice dulls our awareness of the discrepancy. Yet we want to know of prevailing discrepancies so that we can understand the forces really in play and ask relevant questions.

The technique of additive picturing helps us keep our own biases out of the exploration, because it limits the information to pictures based on what the client has said. There is no room to import our own preconceptions. The visual translation forces us to make the information we are receiving tangible rather than abstract.

Moving Toward Clarity

During the consultation, both client and consultant experience a spirit of cooperative learning as objective reality becomes clearer. The greater perspective enables the client to better understand underlying structures and thus what approach might be adopted.

Many managers have used this cooperative learning with the people they manage, and it has enabled the group to rethink many of the assumptions that were built into their companies, divisions, departments, and teams. Then they are able to adjust or redesign as needed.

We can use this thought process ourselves by playing both the client and consultant role. For people just learning this skill, playing both roles can be a bit difficult but, after some experience, new perceptions can be reached.

Greater insight helps in the decision-making process because we can move from thinking about events comparatively to a structural level of understanding in which we see how the various elements within the structure produce consistent patterns of behavior. In my consulting I find that most people begin by using situational and comparative thinking, but later reach valuable structural insights that increase their abilities to deal with complicated issues.

One of the great benefits of structural consulting and the thinking it produces is that a group of people can co-explore reality as easily as an individual. In fact, it is often easier to work with a group because there are more sources of information available, particularly when the exploration is conducted by an experienced structural consultant.

Of course, in the beginning of the exploration everyone has his or her own opinion about reality, and it is usually expressed at an event level. By starting without preconception, then translating information into visual forms, adding the pictures together, sorting out discrepancies, and testing our assumptions, fantastic insights become clear to everyone.

We learn many lessons about the authentic structure that is giving rise to the events we are witnessing, how our actions may or may not contribute to our desired end results, what those desired outcomes are, how to support what matters to us, what our collective values are, how to work together rather than against each other, and much more.

We also incorporate general lessons about the advantages of learning together rather than simply insisting on individual viewpoints. We learn that reality may not be what we assumed it was.

Becoming a Learning Organization

When faced with discrepancy, human beings have an instinct to act. We want to resolve it. Unfortunately, our tendency is to act before we understand. Sometimes, our reactions seem to work, at least temporarily. But too often these actions work against our legitimate longer-term desires.

When we act fast, our feeling is one of control and power. We feel that we are in charge of circumstances and rejoice in our expeditious responses. But our instincts often mislead us. We may act based on inadequate information, perceptions, or habits.

We need to study reality more astutely than we usually do. Not only that, we need to equip ourselves with better instruments for our investigation. Comparative thought processes inherently contain an element in which free association connects points of data and gives us the illusion of deeper understanding.

Some people think that if we deliberate over a longer period of time our results will be more successful. This notion is seldom accurate. Longer deliberation, still using inadequate methods, doesn't significantly alter the ability to penetrate into structures. There is no real difference in jumping to conclusions slowly rather than quickly!

Wisdom does not often express itself through reaction or response, but through a disciplined thought process that allows us to go beyond our previously assumed truths. The same principle is true when we work together in teams and organizations.

When groups of people jump to various conclusions, they may argue with each other about whose conclusion is correct. Little progress is made, but adversity is created. Camps of opinions form and controversies may become political. No one is really to blame, because this type of situation is the natural byproduct of the exclusive use of comparative thinking and the inability to think originally. Anyone faced with the same kind of stimuli and ill-equipped to go beyond old thought process will naturally end up in the same situation.

What makes this type of occurrence more deeply ingrained in our organizations is that often people have created success using these same types of thought processes. It's hard to argue with success. But new situations will not yield to outdated thought processes and time works against us as we attempt to forge a new future.

New challenges are not always addressable through past experiences. So-called open discussions fail to lead to new insights, because merely sharing opinions fails to provide a collective process of exploration. Well-meaning people try their best, but they are left with a cafeteria of opinions and no essential understanding about how they came about.

Though people can point to *aspects* of reality to substantiate their ideas, reality often remains unstudied and unexplored.

People try to change, but too often they are offered only substitutes within the status quo. We are encouraged to change our models, theories, ideals, methods, systems, and views. This type of change does not lead to change of thought process, but merely to variations on the theme of comparison. Progress falters and, unhappily, people return to business as usual.

Learning is inextricably tied to thinking. To attempt to generate a learning organization from an inadequate comparative thought process fails to reach the noble aspirations that are truly desired. We must rethink our processes of thought so that we can learn what we do not currently know. As we master the principles of structural thinking, new ideas become available, new concepts are advanced, and new possibilities are born.

Quick Review

- To create tension in a structural tension system, reality must be viewed objectively.

- Objective reality is not a philosophical concept, but a way of observing reality with perspective and critical accuracy.

- Reality exists independent from our perceptions.

- Comparative thinking uses a personal database of preconceptions, experiences, and ideas with which to compare and categorize reality.

- We often use speculation and assumptions to fill in the gaps in our knowledge. This habit makes it less likely we will ask questions about what we need to know.

- Step one in structural thinking is start without preconception.

- In structural thinking, we explore sets of relationships that generate behavior.

- Thinking structurally involves four phases:

  1. Observation

  2. Study of the relationships formed by observed elements

  3. Structural analysis and conclusions

  4. Working with the structure to redesign as needed

- Structural consultants are those who have been trained in the special skills of structural thinking and structural dynamics.

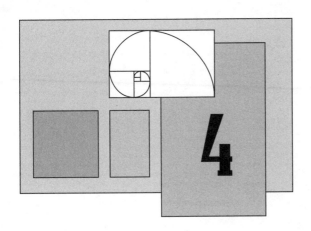

Designs
for
Greatness

CHAPTER 13

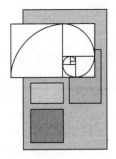

Vision

Part 4 of this book focuses on the building blocks of constructing an organization using a structural approach: vision, leadership, motivation, and learning. We begin in this chapter with the topic of vision, a greatly misunderstood concept within many organizations. Without a vision of the desired states, we cannot achieve most of what we want.

A vision of our desired outcome is one of the two essential elements of structural tension. Without vision, the organization is left to problem-solve its way into an oscillating pattern. But vision cannot be produced by a reaction against what we do not want. It must be a product of what we do want. As we explore the powerful subject of vision, it is good to rethink what it means for an organization to have authentic vision.

The Dynamic Urge

Human beings have various desires that range from altruistic aspirations to base cravings; from selfless inclinations, to survival instincts; from simple appetites, to more complex longings for love, accomplishment, and contribution.

177

Some of these wants seem to arise from the situations in which we find ourselves. But some are independent of the circumstances. There are both situational and non-situational desires.

The non-situational desires may be called our *dynamic urge,* a term that describes our intrinsic desires. The difference between a dynamic urge and a simple situational desire is this: *The dynamic urge is not tied to circumstances, and a situational desire is.* If the circumstances change, a situational desire will disappear, but a dynamic urge will not.

Our dynamic urge is wired into us. We don't choose to have it, we just have it. We can't get rid of it either, although sometimes we may drive it underground in ourselves. We cannot add to it, take away from it, or fake it.

The dynamic urge is a genuine phenomenon of the human spirit in which people, no matter what the circumstances, continue to want to create something that matters to them.

We see the expression of the dynamic urge in the entrepreneur who loves to build businesses. We see it when the great world leaders strive to express values higher than political power and position. We see it in the great artist, scientist, doctor, builder, and athlete.

We see it expressed when those who have been knocked around, defeated, disappointed, and hurt, still try to reach their aspirations. We see it in children when they make pictures, teenagers when they pursue their first driver's license. We see it in adults when their focus is on their deepest values and truest desires.

Organizations, like people, have a form of dynamic urge. This force exists in the purpose of the organization. It is found in the hope people have for the organization. It is a matter of spirit, drive, and energy. We can walk through the corridors of some organizations and feel it.

The organizational dynamic urge cannot be synthetically fabricated. It cannot be manufactured by adopting certain behaviors. It cannot be declared into existence. But it can be observed and felt because the dynamic urge is a *generative* force.

When an organization understands and respects its own generative nature, it is better able to design structures that serve it. And then the organization can advance in the direction it wants to go. The organization can be true to itself.

Frames of the Dynamic Urge

As there are frames of reference by which we observe reality, there are also frames that locate the dynamic urge. To use our metaphor of camera angles, we have a close-up, a medium shot, and a long shot.

In the frames by which we view reality, the medium shot offers us the best vantage point from which to observe reality on the level of object shapes, trends, and patterns. In a similar way, within the dynamic urge, as we will see, the medium shot is the optimal position because it focuses us on our aspirations and values.

When we understand the frames of the dynamic urge, we can do two important things: We can *understand* one of the most important generative forces in the prevailing structure in which we find ourselves, and we can *reposition* the dynamic urge to our best advantage.

Once we survey the frames of the dynamic urge, we will examine how they combine with the reality frames of reference. Structure is the relationship of various elements to each other, and the impact the relationship produces. Structure gives rise to behavior, and the combination of the three frames will demonstrate the behaviors produced by these structural relationships.

The Close-Up.   The-close up shot would focus the dynamic urge toward the immediate, short-term, and instantaneous. This dynamic urge could be seen in the form of appetites on the one hand and survival on the other. Both focus us in the present.

Some people have orientated their lives toward their appetites for food, sex, adventure, pleasure, or whatever. The person experiences time as if it were made up of short, unconnected moments. Within that narrow time frame, the focus is on satisfaction of some immediate stimulation.

When people become obsessed by appetites, it is very hard for them to consider their overriding aspirations or values. Quite often, conflicts between their long-term desires and their short-term appetites lead to feelings of guilt or personal weakness. People who know that their health is threatened by smoking cigarettes, for example, often are convinced they will quit right after "this one last cigarette." The immediate stimulation of the appetite is more compelling than the longer-term aspiration of health.

We might think of appetites as a tension that leads to a quick resolution. The desired state is discrepant with the actual state. And the tension is quickly resolved by indulging in instant gratification.

When we are infants, our desires are instinctive. Food, comfort, warmth, and security are inherent desires that demand immediate satisfaction.

As we mature, our parents do not always fulfill our desires as quickly as they did at first. We begin to realize that there are delays between the initiation of a desire and its fulfillment. Later, as children, we learn that some of the things we want can only be achieved if we are strategic in our actions. If we do save our money instead of buying candy, later we can buy an expensive toy. We learn to delay the resolution of tension to support our more important desires.

This learning is an important part of growing up. We move from an *instinctive* tension-resolution system to a *self-conceived* one. We can begin to think in broader time frames, and this is an important step in the maturation process because it helps us develop the ability to be more effective at creating what matters to us in our lives.

All of us have appetites we would like to satisfy. The question is, do we want to organize our lives around satisfying appetites, or are there other desires that we care about more? A dynamic urge based on appetites is not the foundation for an organization. Nor is it the frame of reference for the members of the organization, especially because professional demands of organizations require long-term discipline to accomplish involved goals.

Survival is another immediate dynamic urge. But, unlike appetites, our focus would shift to survival only if it were in question. If we were in real danger, threatened by war or disease, our dynamic urge would focus us on staying alive. While this dynamic urge is stimulated by the situation, it is not generated by the situation. Therefore, it is not a situational motivation, but a true dynamic urge that is activated when survival is at question.

There may be times an organization faces questions of its own survival. During these times, drastic measures might be adopted to save the company. A vision for the organization may provide a sense of future beyond the current crisis, but survival itself cannot be the organization's vision.

During troubled times people rise to the occasion and deliver extraordinary performances. Wars that threaten a country's survival mobilize people to work together and perform acts of heroism. But, once the war is over and the threat is removed, citizens return to their usual lives. Survival serves its own cause, and cannot serve the cause of a larger aspiration.

Neither appetites nor survival can be the basis of a vision for the organization.

The Long Shot.   People who have a long shot of the dynamic urge have vague hopes and nebulous longings. These people hope that someday their dreams will manifest themselves and bring them happiness and satisfaction. Of course, these desires are so hazy, that they are hard to picture, hard to organize around, and hard to act upon.

We might think the down-to-earth, hard-nosed, real world of organizations is immune to chronic ambiguity, but unfortunately obscurity runs rampant within many organizations. Not only does vagueness appear in the form of mission, purpose, and vision statements, but also in how people use business jargon in their conversations.

The use of jargon is not a shorthand way of making precise points quickly. It is used to obscure meaning. Grandiose-sounding terms may allow people to feel visionary, until the time comes to make a crucial decision, evaluate the implementation of a strategy, choose one technology over another, or review the performance of an employee. Then the vision fades.

Using obscure language is a bad habit. Often these words or phrases originate in some fairly wise concepts, but the concepts have been rendered vacuous by misuse. The word *vision* is such a word, and the phrase *shared vision* is such a phrase.

When an organization does not have clear aspirations it must rely on vague concepts. These concepts have so little substance that they cannot become the basis for a true organizing principle. Because there is room for interpretation, each group may conclude that their notion of the vision is the correct one. They begin to organize around their local interests, and structural conflicts come to prevail.

People know that there is something wrong, but their attempt at a "paradigm shift" may be exceedingly vague. Consequently they cannot get anywhere. Substituting one vague concept for another leaves you with a vague concept.

The Medium Shot. The medium shot of the dynamic urge is well suited to be the dominant organizing principle for the individual and the organization.

All of us have aspirations. The question is, do our aspirations matter enough to us that we would organize our lives or organizations around them?

For great organizations the answer is always yes.

For lesser organizations the answer is no, though they might talk about aspiration and values until they are blue in the face.

This is not to say the desire of these lesser organizations is not real. It is. But they are unwilling to make it the centerpiece of their organization's senior decision-making principle. Instead, they let factors such as the stock market, organizational politics, or prevailing circumstances decide for them if it is okay to want what they want.

While we cannot change the fact that we have dynamic urges, we can focus them. We can move from vague longings or impulsive appetites to our aspirations and values as the primary generative force within our lives and organizations. We can change our frame of reference and when we do we can be clear about what we truly want to create.

Aspirations and Choice

Organizations that are unclear about their aspirations often let their reactions or responses guide the direction of the organization. They react to their industry's market, their competitors' strategies, the fads that become popular, the immediate problems that surface, and so on.

We will always be confronted by challenges and changes in circumstances. The question is this: Are we driven by them, or are we driving our own fate, guided by our highest aspirations and deepest values? When do we know what our true values and aspirations are—when it's convenient, or when it is inconvenient?

An organization chooses its true values and aspirations de facto by the actions it takes, the decisions it makes, and the long-term plans and strategies by which it lives. An organization's choices are the defining moments of its life.

Obviously, when values and benefits are not mutually exclusive, it is easy to pursue them all, but usually we must choose among competing desires. Our choice defines what we value most.

If we say we value innovation while cutting the research and development budget; if we claim to serve our customer, while pursuing ways to cut down on the quality of our products; if we say we want to be a learning organization, while our senior executives never take a course, read a book, or investigate what the other members of the organization think or know; then we are out of touch with reality. We define our real attitudes by our actions, rather than by our claims.

When values and goals are mutually exclusive, we must consciously choose between or among the competing factors. If we don't, structural conflict will become the dominant structure, and we will be driven into a pattern of oscillation. This is an inescapable law of structure. Our choices will tell the real story. The structure will determine the outcome.

We always have this choice: to organize ourselves around our aspirations and values, or not. The history books are filled with tales of great men and women who have chosen their aspirations and values over all other factors, even when it was a hardship to do so.

This choice is not made from a reaction to hype or from a response to the heat of the moment. Often it is a quiet, profound resolve that we come to, and then support by a fundamental choice that we make.

Can an organization succeed without making this type of choice? Sometimes. If it happens to have a wonderful product that people want and no one else has, then the company can still work as a business no matter how dysfunctional the organization is. When you're the only game in town, you can get away with almost anything.

But to say we have vision when we are unwilling to organize ourselves accordingly is self-delusion. To say we have vision when we are afraid to make the hard choices to support the vision is also self-delusion. To say we have vision simply because we *can* envision what we want is also self-delusion.

An organization with clear aspirations and clear values that has chosen to support those qualities through its organizational resolve can discipline its systems to uphold these highest goals. How to make budgetary decisions becomes clear, as do hiring practices, treatment of people, positive and negative consequences, decisions that sort out hierarchies, and so on.

Can the organization use its aspirations and values as a thematic unifying principle? Yes. And all of the great organizations do.

Defining Our Vision

Vision is a word that I helped to make popular. Much of my work in the mid-to-late seventies dealt with people developing vision to help them create the lives they wanted. My first two books, *The Path of Least Resistance* and *Creating*, explored the topic in great depth. I think the subject is tremendously important. But now I'm a bit sorry I helped the term become so prevalent—not because I do not like the notion of vision, but because I do.

The word *vision* has been trivialized to death. Many people in many organizations have discounted vision because it has come to mean vague "Mom and apple pie" statements that never lead to anything substantial. For too many companies, the advantages of real organizational vision has eluded them.

Authentic vision lives, breathes, and is tangible. The term implies *something that we can see well enough to recognize if it appeared in reality.*

Most artists, filmmakers, record producers, architects, interior designers, and other professional creators use vision in their creative process. For them, vision is not nebulous; it is concrete. Many of them could not effectively produce their work if they did not have a well-defined vision. Let's see how it works in the most complicated and organizationally relevant art form—filmmaking.

The scenes of a film are shot out of order, because filmmakers need to shoot all the various scenes that happen at one location before moving on to another location. If films were shot in the order that each scene appeared in the story, it would be a logistical and financial nightmare—going back to the same location and, again, setting up the lights, props, and so on.

The director must have a strong vision of the whole film in his or her mind so that all the parts will eventually fit in with the whole.

There are two elements in particular that the director needs to manage: the performance of the actors, and the technical requirements of camera placement and movement.

Because a film is shot out of sequence, film actors must learn how to jump into a scene as if they were the character going through life in the sequence of the story. Many great actors are able to switch to the right channel when they are asked to perform their scenes. They have a vision of the story, and particularly of their role in it. In this way, they can turn in a performance that moves forward in the *final* product, even though they are performing the scenes out of order.

The director manages all of the actors so that their performances blend together artistically. The director manages the rhythm of the ensemble, pushes the contrasts in certain places, and renders a more subtle effect in other places. Every element is understood in relationship to all the other elements, and the unifying thematic principle is the director's vision of the film.

The other major element that requires a vision of the film is how it is actually shot photographically. The industry standard is to use only one camera. The scene is performed and photographed from many different angles, over and over. The actors perform their parts again and again while the camera shoots the scene from a different position each time.

The actors must perform each take exactly the same way so that the film can be edited together. If an actor has a cigarette in his mouth when he says "Let's look in the closet for the body," he must still have a cigarette in his mouth (and it must be the same brand, the same length, and on the same side of his mouth) when the camera operator moves in for a close-up. The close-up shot may be made three hours after the first shot. Continuity must be maintained by tight management and acute awareness of what has to be matched.

The look and energy of each cut must match the other cuts, so that they will blend together when the film is edited, an exercise that may occur months later.

There are other technical and artistic factors the director must manage, including several crews. Also the director works with other "senior managers"—namely, the cinematographer, the scriptwriter, and the producer. Filmmaking is a collaborative activity, and common understanding of the vision allows people to collaborate.

Without a vision of the end product, the director could not manage the actors and crew. In filmmaking, vision is not a vague notion made up of fuzzy inspirational feelings and sweet-sounding platitudes. It is a profound understanding of the desired state. It is clarity. It is the standard of measurement against which all actions are judged and adjusted. It creates continuity within drastically changing circumstances.

How did it come to pass within our organizations that the notion of vision was reduced to vapidity? Because, like many a good thing, it has been taken on superficially. But, in spite of the misuse of vision over the years, the organization that has real vision has a strength at its disposal.

Clarity of vision is rare in the world of organizations but it is common in the world of the arts. What we can learn from the world of the arts is the *practical* advantages of a real vision properly used.

A vision of the desired end results we are attempting to create is one of the two components of structural tension. The vision might be one about the organization's purpose, or business strategy, or goals that support both. In each case, when we construct a vision we have a solid picture of the desired end result we want to bring into being.

Once a vision has been established, we can observe current reality and notice the discrepancy between the two. *Current reality changes over time, but the vision usually does not.* The vision creates stability in a flurry of activities. Organizations that are unclear about what they are attempting to accomplish will not be able to create structural tension. They will be burdened with structural conflicts as the dominant structure, and they will find themselves in patterns of chronic oscillation.

Now that we have shown how the idea of frames of reference can be used for looking at the dynamic urge and for looking at reality, we can begin to put them together. We want to study their impact on each other as we establish structural tension.

Structural Tension

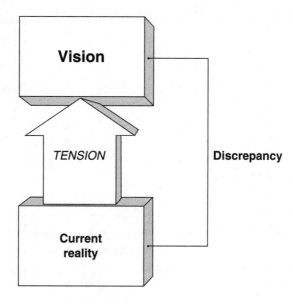

One accurate way to describe structural tension is the relationship formed by the discrepancy between a vision and current reality.

Not all vision is equal. Nor do all views of current reality use the same frame of reference. What follows are all nine possible combinations of structural tension with different frames. As a way of studying the effect of structure, let's examine what tendencies these variations produce; then we can optimize organizational structural tension. First we look at the close-up/close-up combination of frames.

Close Up/Close Up

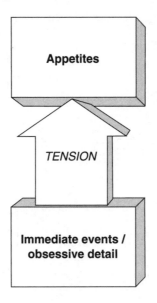

In this combination, the dynamic urge is focused on appetites, and current reality is seen from the perspective of immediate events and/or an obsessive level of detail. Tension leads to quick resolution, as the tendency this structure produces is to pursue ways of gratifying the appetites. If an organization were constituted this way, short-term results and immediate events would dominate the scene. This combination is a difficult one upon which to build a successful company or organization. Unfortunately, we sometimes see this combination when an erratic owner runs a small company. People feel jerked around as each week brings some new direction. The experience of working under such a structure is that everyone exists in a state of chronic frenzy. As a business, success is hard to create because the motivation constantly changes.

While most organizations are not structured like this, some people are. The close-up/close-up combination does not produce a good manager or leader. Now let's look at the close-up/medium shot.

Close Up/Medium Shot

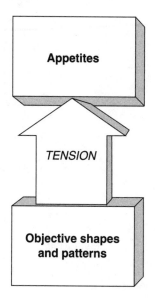

Appetites, combined with an ability to see broader patterns and tendencies, produce an odd combination of traits. One can see the consequences of actions over time, but the drive to gratify appetites immediately seems compelling. If the person's appetite is unhealthy, he or she would know that indulging in it will lead to negative consequences. But the structure will tend to lead the person to indulge anyway.

An organization with such traits could see such qualities as market trends, buying patterns of customers, economic trends, and so on. But the desired state would not give adequate direction to the organization because short-term demands would clash with a clear view of reality.

Close Up/Long Shot

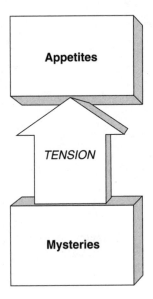

The close-up/long shot is another combination that does not lead to success. A person or an organization would be in a fog, but focused on immediate cravings.

Medium Shot/Long Shot

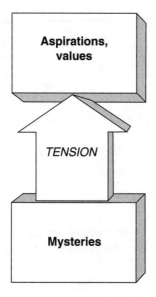

Aspirations and values are the centerpiece of the dynamic urge in the medium shot/long shot combination, but it is hard to get a fix on reality. Because of this, the tension formed is very weak, and unlikely to become the dominant structure for a person or an organization.

Medium Shot/Close Up

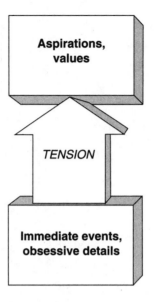

In the medium shot/close-up, while aspirations and values fill the desired state, reality is so narrowly focused that it is hard to evaluate how effective our actions may be. In organizations that have this combination, people pore over mountains of information, hoping that somewhere hidden in the details is useful information. However, they are unable to see what is really going on because their viewpoint is so myopic.

Long Shot/Medium Shot

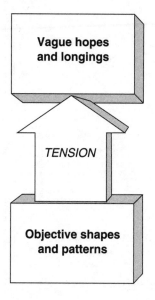

In the long shot/medium shot combination, objective reality is seen and understood, but the dynamic urge is so vague that the tension within the structure is weak. This is a common structure in organizations that substitute platitudes for clarity of vision. Because structural tension is so weak, structural conflicts will eventually dominate the organization.

Long Shot/Close Up

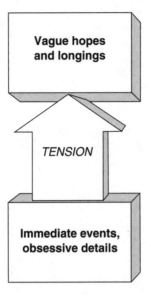

The long shot/close-up is not a winning combination. Vague hopes and obsession with details cause the person or organization to long for things to be better than they are, but the demands of immediate events drive a short-term perception. Again, structural conflict will dominate.

Long Shot/Long Shot

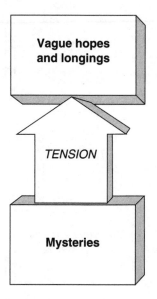

Those with the long shot/long shot combination are lost in space, but optimistic. Occasionally we might run into such a person on a park bench, but never in a board room.

Medium Shot/Medium Shot

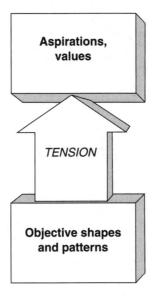

The medium shot of both the vision and the current reality is the best combination for creating structural tension as the dominant force in an individual's life or in an organization. Aspirations and values form the vision of the desired state, and reality is seen objectively and from a wide enough perspective so that shapes, patterns, and tendencies can be understood. Clarity and caring combine to form a critical degree of structural tension, and this can easily become the dominant force in play.

If an individual or an organization changes the frames of reference to a medium shot of both the vision and the current reality, the best possible structure can be formed. This takes discipline, but the activity pays off handsomely.

Authentic Vision

Structural tension is not a gimmick that can be faked. Real vision is not an affectation. Instead, it is an authentic image of the desired end result. The discrepancy between our vision and its relevant current reality forms the most powerful form of structural tension.

A real vision cannot exist when nothing in particular is wanted, no matter how many mental pictures we may form about the future. We cannot have a real vision unless it is based on actual aspiration. However, we do have real aspirations within our dynamic urge. No matter what the circumstances in which we find ourselves, we have the capacity and the inclination to reach for that which is highest and truest in ourselves.

Human beings have authentic aspirations that can become the centerpiece of a person's life. So do organizations. When our organizations are structured to advance, individuals can bring their talents, values, energy, experience, and spirit to bear, and both the members and the organization profit.

Shared Vision

In the world of filmmaking, shared vision is common. Everyone who makes critical decisions that affect the final product must have a common understanding of the vision. Furthermore, they must reinforce the vision through their special professional contribution. The set designer, costume designer, cinematographer, actors, composer, sound designers, props person, script writer, and so on—all are making the same film. From the example of filmmaking we can draw real understanding of what it means to have a shared vision.

An organization with a shared vision is a power to be reckoned with, because when the members of the organization share a common understanding of what they are creating, and a collective caring and commitment to see the vision become a reality, the first element of organizational structural tension is firmly in place. *Shared vision* (on a film set or within an organization) *is the collective dynamic urge that is the prime generative strength that powers the enterprise.*

Because of the challenges filmmakers face—changing weather conditions, changing light conditions, planes going overhead—not all film sets are utopian. But all of the members of the film crew have a strong vision of the film being made. They are committed to its realization both professionally and artistically. Because of their shared vision, everything is tied together. The parts are not seen merely as parts, but as pieces of the whole film that must work together.

Without shared vision, filmmaking would be impossible.

Because of a basic misunderstanding about shared vision in many management circles, its power is often dissipated. Confusion is caused by the erroneous idea that those who share the vision must have some say in its derivation.

When this is the case, shared vision moves from a vision that people share, to a vision that people do *not* share, *unless* they have some say in its formation.

One wonders why someone would be less enthusiastic if they are not part-author of the vision?

In the arts, there is a long tradition of shared vision among professionals—yet it is a vision they did not always shape personally. The first chair violinist does not complain to the conductor, "Hey, I don't know if I want to play this piece by Beethoven unless I can add a few notes!" The actor does not say to the director, "Look, I think this Shakespeare fellow is a little dated in his language. Let me modernize the lingo, so I can really get my teeth in it." These performers are not less able to partake in the vision simply because they did not take a hand in originating it. So why would it be any different for organizations?

In 1961 when John F. Kennedy articulated a vision of safely landing a man on the moon the space program was in its infancy. There was much to do, and a whole world of technology to invent. There were principles to discover and challenges to meet. Tens of thousands of people shared in the Apollo vision. Did they withhold their participation because they did not author the vision in the first place? No, of course not. The members of the Apollo team found many ways to contribute to, and participate in, this vision in which they shared.

Let's end the myth that, for a vision to be shared, people must feel they are authors of it. This myth eliminates the possibility of an authentic shared vision. Not only are some of the most important shared visions in history not a product of a committee, but it is truly *irrelevant* whether the people who help bring the vision into being have anything to do with its creation.

When a vision is truly shared, we participate in it because we care about it, and we will support it through our participation.

If we are willing to withhold or increase our participation based on our degree of authorship, our concern is not really about the vision itself but about *ourselves*. We have shifted our focus from the actual value of the vision, to our own ego involvement. Once this shift takes place, it would be disingenuous indeed to claim a shared vision.

If the vision matters more to us because we had a hand in creating it, then the vision's intrinsic value must be in question, or we have our focus in the wrong place.

When we truly care about the vision, it matters little who originated it.

A playwright was asked how he chose the directors of his plays. His answer was "I have the director tell me the story of my play. If he tells me the story I wrote, we can work together. If he doesn't, we can't, because everyone on stage needs to be telling the same story."

Imagine everyone in an organization telling the same story—by the actions they take and the ways they handle themselves professionally. Imagine that they share a common understanding of the direction the organization is going, and imagine that they care about the organization reaching its goals and manifesting its vision. Anytime we dealt with anyone from that organization, we would get a sense of a company that had a shared vision, one that deeply mattered to them.

The Great Vision

Shared vision is a powerful unifying principle for an organization or a movement. But not all visions are equal. A vision that captures the imagination is one that has the ability to move people to positive action.

A great vision engenders great participation, because of the eighth law of organizational structure.

THE EIGHTH LAW OF ORGANIZATIONAL STRUCTURE

The values that dominate an organization will displace other competing, lesser values.

It is an inescapable law of organizational structure that the values that dominate an organization will displace competing but lesser values. The greater the value, the lower the likelihood that lesser values will be taken into account, or be influential.

In light of true greatness, pettiness disappears. When individuals or organizations are pursuing great accomplishments, many of the trivial concerns that might otherwise have been distracting are no longer relevant within the context of their aspiration.

This eighth law of organizational structure cuts two ways, however. If the dominant values of an organization are self-serving, political, and manipulative, then what is trivial will become more important than the accomplishment of a great cause. When pettiness is a dominant value, true greatness disappears.

Greatness can be measured, not simply by size or power, but by scope and character. When confronted by greatness as a dominant value, the organization has something by which to measure and judge every aspect of the enterprise. Is what we are doing consistent with our aspiration and vision? If it is not, we are ready to consider what types of structural changes we need to make. We not only tolerate change, we actively seek it. In light of true greatness, change and restructuring become naturally motivated. As we become clear about the vision we share, we can join together in making change work.

Shared Vision and Choice

When people join together in a common cause, each person makes an individual choice to participate. There is tremendous power in the act of making a choice, for it defines our personal resolve and our intended direction.

The choice to support a vision that reaches beyond the individual's personal gain makes possible feats that would otherwise be improbable. This type of choice reflects that which is highest in the spirit of humanity—choosing to join together and work together.

The importance of this choice is that it defines our motivation. If we had no real choice, we could only go to our destiny cooperatively, or kicking and screaming.

When we are forced into participation, we may withhold our

fullest involvement as a kind of rebellion. It is our nature to resist manipulation, mendacity, and coercion.

When the intention of any action is to manipulate us, we rebel. We may do it subtly, or in the privacy of our own mind, or we may do it publicly. But we do it. We do it to affirm our own independence of spirit.

The introduction of many well-intentioned ideals backfires when organizations attempt to use them to manipulate their members into higher performance or greater allegiance. The members withhold their involvement to some degree, and then there is a breakdown of the relationship between the individual members of the organization and the organization itself.

Some organizations have used the ideal of shared vision to manipulate people into thinking that they have more say in the decisions and direction of the organization than they actually do. When this is the case, people are less likely to support the aims of the organization, not because of the level of their decision-making power, but because they resent the attempt to manipulate people into compliance.

When organizations tout values that they do not support in deeds and design, the hypocrisy becomes transparent to the members of the organization. When this is done in the name of shared vision, the ploy drives people to look out for their own interests.

When organizations *do* support their values in what they do and how they do it, the possibility for true greatness moves from the level of an abstract ideal to actual reality. Think of the greatness of vision of such companies as Microsoft, Sony, Disney, Turner Broadcasting, Cannon, and many others. While some of these companies have merged to become bigger players on the world scene, and others simply grow and grow, one factor that makes them great is their shared vision. Without a shared vision, their growth strategies would fail. Their vision becomes the focal point of their structural advancement based on structural tension. They know where they want to go, they know where they are in relationship to their vision, and they take strategic steps to move toward their vision.

On the other hand, growth is not the only sign of a true focus on a shared vision. When AT&T shocked the world in the fall of 1995 by voluntarily dividing into three separate companies, bucking the bigger-is-better merger trend, they were guided by a real understanding of the differing visions that existed. They understood that these three visions did not combine to make one larger vision. By splitting the company, AT&T believed that it would be able to create organizations that serve each vision in a focused way. In the highly competitive world of telecommunications, AT&T had the wisdom to understand the power of sharing a vision within the frame of their aspirations and strategies. They were able to demonstrate that the organization is there to serve the vision, rather than the other way around.

The Spirit of a Vision Shared

When people share a common vision, they can perform feats that would otherwise be impossible. They can put all of their actions into the same context, and they can align themselves in the same direction. However, even beyond the great advantages that a shared vision provides, is the power of the act itself.

There is something in the human spirit that longs for participation with others, that wants to be involved in a collective endeavor. Sometimes we find this spirit expressed on the level of a project team within a large organization. The members of the team are able to work together in ways that are reminiscent of the greatest Olympic sports teams. Sometimes we see this spirit expressed in the wider organization. The organization takes on a life force that is truly extraordinary— a spirit that moves beyond simply doing a good job to doing something that deeply matters. These people seem to carry their own generative energy as their collective dynamic urge is given full voice.

Shared Structural Tension

Even more potent than shared vision is shared structural tension. The vision is the desired state. People join together to bring the vision into being. The vision forms a context by which to review reality. Dedication to the vision is just one component of shared structural tension. One of the other factors is the ability of the organization to deal objectively with reality in its evaluations and implications. We can see what is relevant to study in reality. We can observe the tendencies and patterns. We can learn from our successes and failures. We can innovate our processes as needed, and when needed. We can develop the overall capacity to manage the entire enterprise quickly, flexibly, and effectively.

Vision or shared vision without structural tension will eventually lead to wider oscillation when the organization is dominated by structural conflicts. But when shared structural tension is the dominant structure, we can grow, not only in size, but in competency, ability to learn, ability to invent, and the vital ability to discipline all of the organization's systems to support the common direction and purpose.

Quick Review

- Vision is one of the two elements that form structural tension. An organization that lacks vision will not be able to create structural tension, and will eventually oscillate.

- The dynamic urge is our desires that are non-situational; we want what we want independently from the circumstances.

- Organizations have a form of dynamic urge.

- The dynamic urge can have a close-up, medium-shot, or long-shot frame of reference.

- A medium-shot framing of current reality and vision is the best combination to create strong structural tension.

- An organization that is unclear about its aspirations often lets its reactions or responses to prevailing circumstances guide its direction.

- Great organizations use aspirations and values as a thematic unifying principle.

- The eighth law of organizational structure is: **The values that dominate an organization will displace other competing, lesser values.**

- Shared vision is a collective dynamic urge that is the prime generative force that powers a successful organization.

- A shared vision need not be derived by all those that share and participate in the vision.

- Shared structural tension is a more powerful generative force than a shared vision.

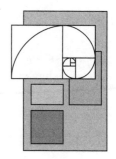

CHAPTER 14

Leadership

We now examine one of the most important building blocks of a well-structured organization: leadership. In this chapter we can explore the function of leadership from a structural perceptive.

Great leaders are rare, and even rarer within organizations. This is a pity, because strong and clear leadership is a vitally important element within the structural makeup of any organization. With it, the organization can focus its efforts toward a common direction, align its collective actions, and adjust and learn over time. Without it, the organization will tend to oscillate as people from different departments are forced to find their own ways without clear direction and guidance. Often this situation gravitates toward entrenched conflicts of interests, uninvolvement, and confusion.

When issues cannot be decided; when underfunded projects limp on without clear support; when department heads fight it out over the same resource base; when strategies are unclear and various tactics cancel each other out; when decisions are made and then unmade; when the word of the organization is suspect, and every attempt to better conditions seem like a desperate struggle to overcome inertia; in all of these situations we see telltale signs of the absence of real leadership. Would a strong leader eradicate these patterns of behaviors? Yes, without doubt.

But what are the elements of leadership?

Elements of Leadership

Clarity

The result of true leadership within an organization is clarity. People understand what there is to do and why it is important to do it. They also want personally to support the organization's vision and values by translating them into action. They are involved and they care.

Clarity does not just happen to an organization. It is consciously and carefully created by a leader who begins with personal clarity. Clarity of vision and clarity of objective reality are essential. A clear strategy that supports and expands viability, such as the business strategy, is fundamental.

Total Responsibility

The leadership role is special, in that leaders take *total* responsibility for the organization. While there is much talk these days about "stakeholders" and "ownership" as factors that cause members of the organization to be more involved and more committed, the leader is still the person who must carry the leadership burden totally. While the leader might encourage others to feel as deeply about the purpose of the organization, drive their actions with as much fire and commitment, bring to light new ideas and processes that help the cause, be as participatory as the leader is, the success of the enterprise still falls on the leader's shoulders. Those in leadership positions who do not understand this principle are bound to end up as victims of circumstances, or victims of inadequate structures.

Substance, Not Style

While it has become popular to promote a "softer, gentler" style of leadership, style is not the essence of leadership. The essence of leadership is substance, including wise judgment, strength of character, clarity of purpose, and a generative nature with a strong dynamic urge toward values and aspirations.

For the most part, leadership *styles* are irrelevant. Those who encourage consensual participation and those who are autocratic can be effective leaders, or not. The style or approach will not be a factor in true leadership, although when true leadership is absent, many people fill the vacuum by talking about leadership style.

We may love the style of a leader, but not join in. We may hate the style of a leader, but feel honored to participate within the organization. Leaders who attempt to win popularity contests often fall victim to the wrong values, such as doing what is fashionable rather than what is right.

Beyond Personality

When we think about great leaders, we conjure the likes of Martin Luther King, Jr., Winston Churchill, Mahatma Ghandi, John F. Kennedy, and other charismatic personalities who were able to capture the imagination of millions of people. In our television age, leadership appears to be tied to celebrity status. But this impression is inaccurate, particularly in organizational leadership.

Organizational leadership requires neither the magnetism of an extraordinary television personality nor the mystique of a historic figure. Some of the most effective organizational leaders might not stand out in a crowd or thrill the multitudes merely by their presence. Nonetheless, they are able to inspire in others a profound desire to join together and build a desired future. Bill Gates of Microsoft is a good example of such a leader. His "charisma" (if it might be said he has any) is not a product of personality, but a truly majestic vision about the future of computerization and electronics. He also has a well-developed and judicious ability to assess reality, and he has mastered his business strategy. He is enormously generative, with a strong dynamic urge focused on values and aspirations. He takes a stand for his aims. You get the feeling from him that he is going to go to his destination no matter what the circumstances, and you are invited to join him if you want to get involved.

Leadership and Structural Tension

One of the most important aspects of *real leadership is the ability to establish structural tension as the dominant structure within the organization.* Leadership is inextricably tied to the structural makeup of the organization. If the underlying organizational structure is inadequate, the leader must work to change it.

Peter Senge has made the point that we often think of a leader as captain of the ship, commander of the troops, the person in charge of big decisions. Filled with vision for the future, energy to meet the challenge, and personal magnetism to engage the masses, he or she forges distinct and divergent parts into a well-conceived whole. But, as Peter adds, there is another image of leadership with a less mythical tradition that is just as compelling: the leader as architect and designer of the organization's structure.

Who has more real influence over performance? The captain of the ship or the ship's designer?

Leadership does require a captain, of course. Decisions need be made, the course set, and the crew instructed. But the best leaders are also involved with elements of design. A leader who thinks structurally can determine the desired outcomes *and* design the vehicle used to achieve the vision.

The organization is not unlike a ship. It is a vehicle conceived for transport. It seeks to travel from point to point through time and space—from smaller to larger markets, from simple businesses to more complex businesses, from local to worldwide engagement. But organizations have a distinct advantage over ships. They can be redesigned en route to their destinations. Structural tension is the key to the best structural design, because a true leader is guided by a vision, is fluent in the actual state of reality in relationship to the vision, and is able to manage the process by which the organization moves toward its goals. Not only that, the true leader is able to position structural tension throughout the organization as the dominant structure. All great leaders use structural tension, some with *conscious* competence, others with *unconscious* competence. In either case, they all practice it.

Would we follow a leader who did not have a vision of a desired future? Would we follow a leader who was out of touch with reality? Would we follow a leader who did not know how to guide our collective efforts to our desired state? No, of course not.

There are other aspects of leadership we will explore later in this chapter, but the above factors are essential. *The lack of any **one** of these factors would compromise a person's ability to lead.*

THE GREAT LEADER

All great leaders have had these traits:
- They knew where they wanted to go (the desired end result)
- They knew where they currently were
- They deeply cared about the end result
- They were able to encourage others to join them in creating the result
- They were able to help others focus on reality in relationship to the desired end result
- They were able to translate structural tension into actions that were designed to move from current reality to the desired outcome

---

A Sterling Example

One of the great leaders of the twentieth century was Martin Luther King, Jr. Many personal aspects of this exceptional individual contributed to his strength of character, and one of them was his mastery of what we now understand to be structural tension. In his famous *I Have a Dream* speech, we see a masterpiece of structural tension in the way Dr. King tied the original founding *vision* of the United States, freedom of the individual and justice for all, to actual contemporary conditions—*current reality*. Toward the end of the speech, Dr. King further developed the vision of freedom and justice with these lines, "Although we face the difficulties of today and tomorrow, I still have a dream. It is a dream deeply rooted in the American dream . . . "

Structural tension was present in much of Dr. King's work, including his monumental *Letters from a Birmingham Jail*, which is one of the most persuasive documents ever written in favor of freedom, justice, and the dignity of humanity. *Letters* was another of Dr. King's works that positions vision in relationship to the current situation of the day.

Dr. King was neither a business leader nor a senior manager of a large organization. But we can see in him something that every organizational leader needs—an ability to articulate a deeply felt vision, a vision steeped in the highest of values, filled with true aspiration, and describing reality accurately and objectively. In addition the leader also needs an ability to take a stand for his or her vision in light of strong opposition.

Taking a Stand

Most business leaders are not required to confront the moral and physical challenges that Martin Luther King faced. But they encounter moral questions of their own. How can they support the actual vision and direction of the organization in light of the many pressures on them to do otherwise? They are required to take a stand for the organization in the form of the choices they make, the policies they design, and the ways they structure the organization.

Too often, people in leadership positions fail to make the hard choices. They might attempt to "balance" competing factors such as long-term growth investment strategies and short-term financial performance, but these choices neutralize each other and it is impossible for the organization to serve either one adequately.

The leader needs to determine which of the competing factors is the most important, and then support that one over the others. Not everyone will be happy with the choice, but it must be made, and then reinforced by the series of secondary decisions that support it. The leader must take a stand for the chosen direction.

When it is necessary to take a stand, some people in leadership roles avoid the "moment of truth" and attempt diplomacy instead. If a leader does not decide which competing goals are the most important, *none* of the goals will be adequately satisfied or supported. Members of the organization will not know how to address the many critical issues they face. Each side will think its approach is the correct one. They will think that if the other side were more understanding of the "real situation" there would be agreement to support the "correct" approach (which happens to be their own approach).

As a consequence of weak leadership, the organization is left directionless and everyone suffers. In one pharmaceutical company, for example, senior management failed to decide whether to support virology research as their R&D strategy. Some members of the company thought much of the future success of the business lay in virology, but others thought their competitors had a better command of virology research; just to play catch-up would be an enormous investment, putting them in a "me too" position without market or scientific superiority or control.

The issue was discussed endlessly. But no real decision was ever made. Virology looked like a good bet some months and a bad one other months. People in research continued to explore virology compounds. When they had developed something that was ready to enter the FDA clinical-trial process, the clinical group responsible for the trials was unprepared to handle the workload. They didn't have the staff, the funding, or, as far as they knew, the corporate mandate. A conflict developed between the R&D department and clinical research. At first the cause of the conflict looked like personality problems between rival groups of strong-willed scientists. To people in clinical research, the R&D people seemed like a group of mavericks who were manipulating the system; to the R&D people, clinical research seemed to be thwarting their important work. Conflict-resolution techniques were tried, but, as we might expect, they failed to address the real issue.

The real issue was this: Because of the leadership vacuum, people created their own sense of direction based on their understanding of what the corporation was trying to accomplish. Each side in this dispute continued to wonder why the other side was being so unreasonable and uncooperative. Until this issue was driven upward, forcing senior management to make a final decision about virology, the conflict was unaddressable.

This example points to a chronic pattern within many corporations. Leadership fails to set adequate direction, so those on other levels of the organization compensate by setting their own direction. The results always lead to structural oscillation. This is because of the ninth law of organizational structure.

THE NINTH LAW OF ORGANIZATIONAL STRUCTURE

> # When a senior organizing principle is absent, the organization will oscillate.

Without a higher-order organizing principle such as structural tension, an organization will self-organize into various structural conflicts as various groups try to do a good job. Even cross-functional teams cannot help when an organizing principle is absent. The teams may attempt to create their own senior organizing principle, but if their efforts are not supported by those in leadership positions, the attempt will be neutralized. The consequence will be a return to structural oscillation.

A story that reflects this principle in the extreme is William Golding's *Lord of the Flies*, in which a group of English choirboys are stranded on a tropical island. They quickly divide into various groups. The situation becomes more threatening over time as some groups struggle against the others for dominance.

When Golding wrote this tale during the late fifties, in the midst of the Cold War, many saw it as a cynical metaphor for East-West relations. Beyond the politics of the era, the story of what happened to this group of boys when there was no senior organizing principle in effect does have haunting similarities to many modern organizations. Of course, the behavior within most organizations is more civilized and the conflicts are more subtle than Golding's choirboys were. But the pattern of fragmenting into competing groups is often much too similar.

Golding's story ends when a naval officer comes onto the island. His presence ends the combat between rival groups. In the presence of a senior organizing principle (the naval officer), order is restored. Among the other requirements of the job, leaders must establish the senior organizing principles so that the organization can advance in its chosen direction.

The Principle of Hierarchy

As was said, exceptional leadership produces organizational clarity. The key to clarity is the principle of hierarchy, and leaders must establish and reinforce it throughout the organization. As we have seen in Chapter 6, hierarchy is the key to redesigning structural conflicts. This is one reason that leaders must understand the structural conflicts that exist within their organizations and be able to use hierarchy as a power force to create structural tension.

The organization needs to know from its leaders what is *more* important and what is *less* important, be it on the level of values, goals, strategies, policies, or functions.

If we didn't make hierarchical distinctions, we would need to conclude that everything we do is of equal importance. When everything is equal, nothing stands out and all factors become arbitrary.

Certainly the organization's purpose takes the highest place in relationship to all other factors. Even questions of viability are secondary to purpose, because if an organization doesn't have a reason to exist, viability is irrelevant.

After purpose comes viability, because if an organization cannot fund itself, it cannot support its purpose. This is why the business strategy is so important. But a business strategy without supporting management systems to reinforce it is difficult to implement. And if management is not tied to the business strategy, it will lack direction. "Good" management designs created in a vacuum that conflict with the business strategy are harmful to the health and well-being of the organization. Thus when an organization adopts the latest management fad, it will almost always find that the new process doesn't work in its shop.

The relationship between business strategy and management strategy is one area where direction from leadership is absolutely essential—and where it is often missing, to the disadvantage of the organization.

Leadership must master the business strategy. Without that dimension, it would be impossible to direct the collective efforts of the organization. But the trend in many companies is to ignore or misunderstand their own business strategy and, instead of focusing on how the company *generates* wealth, put their attention on financial management—how the company *accumulates* wealth.

The business strategy is concerned with how we get money to come in the door. Those charged with financial matters are concerned with how money is spent after it comes in the door. Without a hierarchy established between the two points of view, a structural conflict will emerge as the dominant structure. The business strategy will be driving the organization to align proper resources to workload demands in order to build the business. When those driving the strategy incur costs as part of their investment in governing the ratio between workload and capacity, those who are attempting to accumulate wealth will become alarmed that the organization is spending too much on resources. They will then look for areas that can be cut. But, once the cuts are made, the organization is less able to generate new wealth because of its unmet capacity needs. Eventually, more capacity is added to make up for what has been cut, and the cycle of oscillation begins once again.

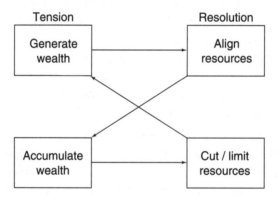

Whenever we see exercises in across-the-board percentage downsizing, we know that the business needs are not being properly considered or addressed. An organization that cuts 10 or 20 percent of its capacity indiscriminately does not comprehend its actual capacity costs, or what it needs to grow. What would we think if a surgeon said to us that we need to downsize 20 percent of our body through surgery? Wouldn't we want to know exactly which 20 percent was under consideration, and what would be the function of surgery? Would we think that the surgeon had considered our health and well-being adequately, or would we think that the doctor was a lunatic?

Certainly, if the organization has not managed its capacity costs well, it is important to make adjustments. Where does it have excess capacity that needs to be cut or shifted? Where does it need to invest in capacity to make it adequate?

We could never consider a mindless percentage cut if we were truly aligning resources toward our business strategy, for to do so would be completely illogical and potentially disastrous to the fundamental constitution of the company. And yet, unfortunately, we continue to see senseless downsizing. Those in leadership positions are being terribly foolish when they allow this to happen to their organizations.

Conflict Manipulation

The failure of leadership to establish business hierarchy is often supported by consultancy firms that specialize in extreme downsizing measures. In an act of organizational irresponsibility, a leader can claim that he or she is only doing what the high-priced experts have advised. When leadership abdicates its role, the magnitude of structural oscillation widens.

The tactic of attempting to force managers to perform better because their jobs are threatened is a manipulation of the management system. Emotional conflicts and fear of negative consequences are used to mobilize the remaining members of the organization. People learn to hide, procrastinate, and create counter manipulations. The pattern produces lower actual performance.

Structural consultant Chloe Cox spoke about one of her UK clients, a manufacturing plant that was part of a large international company:

> Just at the point that they needed new investment to expand their capacity, their U.S. parent company cut their budget while asking them to increase their capacity. The cuts were made in a vacuum, and people felt under the gun, and reacted by creating schemes to demonstrate their worth so the parent wouldn't make further cuts. Consequently, they "bungee

jumped" from one change management process to another. From visioning workshops, to quality improvement process, to employee development programs, to whatever was the latest fad. When we began to work with the plant, they were just beginning to look at the topic of *complexity*. The sad thing was that none of their attempts were likely to work. The plant management became more powerless with each new initiative. Here was a case where the leadership in the parent company seemed completely lost, and the rest of the organization was left to fend for itself. Until we confronted top management about the conflict of goals they were initiating, progress couldn't be accomplished for the plant.

In one organization, a large telecommunication company, the process of systematic cuts and heightened antagonism from senior management drove their best people to other companies. The remaining people in the company were taught to use the phrase *burning platform* to describe how conflict was being used to manipulate people into higher performance. The concept was that each person and each team was standing on a platform that was burning up. Time was running out, and if the individual or team did not accomplish what was required they would be consumed by fire. The only escape was to jump to a higher platform. Once the new platform was reached, it would begin to burn. This image was designed to create a sense of urgency.

Manipulation and Structure

The structure that is formed by this tactic is identical to that of problem solving, but its effects are even more disruptive to an organization. Let's analyze this method from a structural point of view.

First, conflict is established by threatening the individual members of the organization:

When the conflict reaches a critical point, the person reacts against the conflict by taking action. The motivation for the action is to reduce the intensity of the emotion the person is experiencing—the emotion caused synthetically by the conflict:

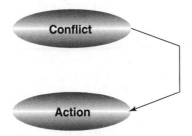

So far, the manipulation seems to have worked because the person has jumped into action. But in the next part of the cycle the action reduces the intensity of the conflict:

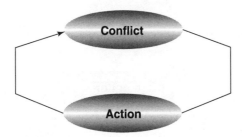

Since the conflict motivated the person to act, less conflict leads to less action. The illustration on page 218 shows a structural mechanism that I have termed *conflict manipulation*. It is a common ploy practiced by many to use pressure, guilt, fear, threats, and various images of negative outcomes to force people into action.

Managers who use conflict manipulation are able to create short-term results. But once the experience of conflict is reduced and the heat is off, people return to their previous patterns of performance. The nature of the structure is self-defeating, in that the impetus for action is always reduced by any action that has been taken, whether or not it really works to better the situation. Soon afterwards, new pressure has to be introduced. New threats, fear tactics, and images of disaster will drive a new period of action, but the structural function of the action reduces the intensity of the conflict.

The intensity of the conflict is reduced because the person feels more in control as a result of the action taken, and this change of experience leads to even less future action.

At first, the conflict the manager introduces has shock value. But

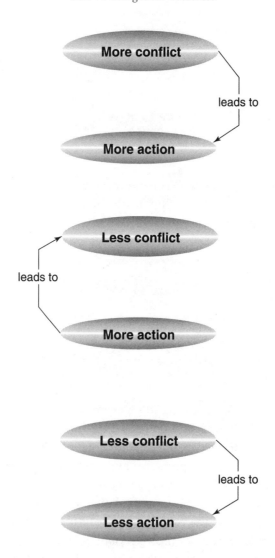

after this pattern cycles through a few times, people begin to expect it. Cries that the sky is falling no longer have the emotional impact they once had, and people become unmotivated to react. A manager using conflict manipulation must increase the sense of disaster over time just to create the equivalent degree of reaction that the people once felt, and eventually they become entirely desensitized to hysterics. A predictable pattern of oscillation develops as the magnitude sometimes widens, sometimes diminishes, and everyone eventually under-performs.

Leadership cannot be based on conflict manipulation for two important reasons. First, it takes more and more conflict to produce the same *declining* performance. Those using this tactic eventually lose credibility as they become increasingly more fervent. Second, one must distort reality, exaggerating it if it is not "bad enough" to produce a suitable amount of conflict. This puts the leader in the untenable position of having to misrepresent reality and destroy one of the two pillars of structural tension. If the leader becomes an unreliable source of data about objective reality, credibility is lost.

Fair and Unfair Games

People do not play fairly in an unfair game. Many organizations are devised like unfair games, and so one very important function of leadership is to make sure that the organization is set up fairly. Are people able to succeed based on the merits of their efforts, or are they subject to organization politics, power issues, or mindless bureaucracies? Does the reward system reinforce the organization's values, or does it contradict them?

If a leader is attempting to create a high-performance organization capable of innovation, critical thinking, organizational learning, professionalism, and increasing competence, he or she must make sure that the foundation for such an organization is a fair game. If it isn't, the leader will sound disingenuous when articulating the vision, talking about the future, revealing plans for redesigning the company, announcing new goals, or speaking of the organization's values. People will read the leader's declarations in relationship to the reality they see before them. If they are being encouraged to do more with fewer resources while senior management has just given itself an enormous raise in salary; or if they are encouraged to become a learning organization when senior management seems set in its ways and unable to learn anything; or if quality is declared to be an important value while the organization promotes business as usual; then leadership will be seen as hypocritical, and no one will take the leader's affirmations seriously. People will learn that to succeed within the company one needs to manipulate the system better than anyone else.

In some cases, the leadership faces a structural conflict between personal gain and organizational gain, an absolutely terrible situation. Within this structure, a person in a prime leadership role (such as CEO or managing director) owns equity in the company. The performance of the stock prices impacts this person's personal wealth. Perhaps this person is going to leave the company in two or three years, and plans to sell the stock at that time. For some people, their personal gain becomes senior to anything else, including the organization.

There are some who have managed their company's stock performance to the detriment of the organization's long-term ability to perform in its industry, making decisions designed to sway Wall Street rather than to support needed growth and expansion. This type of person always claims that his or her decision is for the good of the company, but the real motivation is transparent to the other members of the organization who must attempt to make the company work in spite of unwise policies. In the aftermath of such leadership, the company pays dearly in terms of losing business, being able to compete, having to use catch-up growth tactics, and having to rebuild the constitution of the business after the person leaves the company. There are too many examples of people in leadership roles managing their personal gain rather than the health and well-being of the organization, leaving it in shambles, and leaving other members to pick up the pieces. This is an unfair game against which boards of directors must be vigilant.

Machiavellian values aside, other organizational and business-related structural conflicts often become the basis for organizational unfairness. People work against their own personal values and aspirations. Often an unfair game is the outcome of an inadequate structure. This is another reason why addressing the structure of an organization is paramount; a change from structural oscillation to structural advancement can determine whether the members of the organization participate fully. Leadership must be aware of the impact of the inescapable laws of organizational structure and redesign the organization as needed.

Within a poorly structured organization, leadership is the last court of appeal for true change, because transformation of the organization's structure will not happen unless leadership generates it personally. Within a well-structured organization, leadership helps drive change from a structural rather than a situational point of view. A well-structured organization is a fair game, and the probability for organizational and individual advancement becomes very high indeed.

The Leader as Leader

True leadership is a combination of elements. Some of these elements are on the level of skills, and others are on the level of personal character. Leaders must understand the relationship of the parts to the whole. Without such understanding, the leader is bound to make faulty decisions that emanate from situational thinking. With structural understanding, the leader can focus the organization on issues of interconnectedness and structural design.

The leader must be able to lead both technically and spiritually. The spirit of the organization, based on its founding purpose, its values, and its aspirations, must be supported and reinforced by actions. The words must be consistent with the actions. The leader must take a stand in favor of the organization, and infuse the organization with the desire to accomplish its aims. This situation cannot be created on an unsound foundation, so the organization must also become a fair game that rewards performance, not politics.

If the leader does not carry these traits and abilities within his or her own being, it will be difficult for the organization to follow. Clarity of direction, purpose, structure, and spirit begin with the leader's own resolve, and cannot be faked. In leadership, truth will win out over illusion and substance will succeed over manner.

Real leadership requires a certain height and depth, strength of character, and strong dynamic urge. When these factors are in place, great accomplishments can be achieved.

Quick Review

- Leadership is a critical element in organizational structure. With it, the organization can focus on its aims. Without it, the organization will gravitate towards structural conflicts leading to oscillation.

- Clarity is a result of true leadership.

- Leadership is not influenced by style but by substance.

- Leaders establish structural tension within the organization. They need to be clear about the organization's aspirations and its current reality.

- Leaders are confronted by various moral questions. They are required to take a stand for the organization's values and aspirations, and to decide between competing interests.

- When leadership is weak within an organization, other members compensate by supporting their own local interests. This forms structural conflicts.

- The ninth law of organizational structure is: **When a senior organizing principle is absent, the organization will oscillate.**

- The key to a leader's clarity is the principle of hierarchy, and leaders must establish and reinforce clarity throughout the organization.

- Attempting to lead by conflict manipulation leads to oscillation and loss of credibility.

- It is the leader's job to set up a fair game, one in which people are rewarded on their own merits.

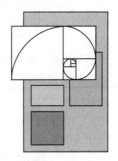

CHAPTER 15

Motivation

Another important building block in structural redesign is motivation. This chapter looks at key factors that can lead either to real involvement or to limited participation within the organization.

Why do people do what they do? What is their motivation? The way an organization answers these questions will lead to specific organizational policies and practices that will have enormous impact on how the organization operates. The organization's understanding of motivation can lead either to structural tension or structural conflicts—to structural advancement or structural oscillation.

Without understanding what truly motivates people to reach for that which is highest and best in them, organizations design rewards that actually work against people's intrinsic motivation. To what degree can the organization bring out best performance? Should the organization be concerned with the motivation of its members?

If the organization doesn't consider its members' motivation, structural conflicts can develop that pit the individual against the organization. This is a conflict all organizations would rather live without. Structure has an important role in motivation, not because structure can generate motivation in a vacuum, but because a well-structured organization is a place where individuals are able to grow, learn,

223

develop, contribute, and work with others. In a poorly structured organization, even the best, most capable people are working against the forces in play. As people learn to compensate for chronic oscillation, it becomes impossible to bring out their personal best.

Two Forms of Motivation

The most powerful motivator for both the individual and the organization is a desire to create a result—*just so that the result can exist.* As Robert Frost said, "All the great things are done for their own sake."

This is not how we have been taught to think. Instead, we have been taught to think in terms of personal "return on investment." When we do something, we have learned to ask what the payback will be. But human beings often have higher motives than self-focused ones, and an individual, a leader, or an organization can tap into those higher motivations and involve people without manipulation or emotional bribes. We can join together in an action of free will and true choice.

Focus on the Doer

Consider the following illustration:

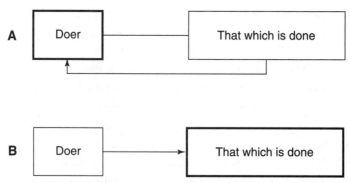

In the first diagram (A), the focus is on the doer. The point of participation is to provide the person with a return on the investment of his or her time, energy, and action. The return might be material or emotional or both. Nonetheless, the payback functions identically, in that *the person takes part in order to be compensated.*

This is the most common idea about motivation in our society: We do what we do for a return on investment. Television and magazine ads show us how wonderful we will look and feel if we use their company's products. Success, satisfaction, riches, admiration, and love are some of the prizes these ads promise to the potential buyer. The assumption built into the message is simple: Life is dedicated to your enjoyment.

No one likes to be a fool, and so, when we have been taught to think in terms of "what's in it for me," we adopt this notion as a natural value. After all, society tells us that our reward is a symbol of our intelligence and savvy. Smart people are supposed to be cleverly motivated by how well their actions balance costs-benefit ratios (the cost of their effort versus the benefits they receive).

There doesn't seem to be a socially acceptable way of describing altruistic motivations. When we do try, we can look like empty-headed idealists. To avoid this image, we may be tempted to list the personal benefits we are receiving in everything we do. We find ourselves trying to communicate the message that we are not fools or dreamers, but rather down-to-earth individuals who know enough to look out for Number One. We would rather be seen as opportunistic than utopian.

Now, there is nothing intrinsically wrong with looking out for Number One. Nor is there anything wrong with being concerned with a return on investment. If we were investing money in a new financial scheme, probably ROI would be the driving force behind our activity. However, the scope of our participation would be limited to how well we thought the project would pay us back. Since we could not know for sure if the investment would succeed until the final returns were in, we would have to speculate about its prospects. We would attempt to forecast how well it might reward us, and then ask ourselves if getting involved would warrant our participation.

In this orientation, we would not be able to be involved fully with what we are doing because, if our perceptions changed about how good the return on investment was, our level of involvement would have to change accordingly.

Looking now at the second diagram (B) of the illustration, we see that *we participate because of that which is being done.* Not only do we care about the outcome of our actions, *the outcome itself motivates us.*

Those of us who have children know this type of motivation well. We take them to dance class or baseball practice, not so they will become rich and famous and make us proud, but because we love them. We take care of them when they are sick, not because we hope that they will take care of us when we are old and gray, but because we love them. We involve ourselves in their lives, not to manipulate them into symbols of our good parenting so we can feel good about ourselves, but because we love them. Our focus is on *them*, not us. The point of our actions is to support them in ways that are independent of rewards.

Is this principle translatable to the corporate world? Yes. The consummate professional is motivated by a commitment to a desired outcome. "I play the game for the sake of the game," Sherlock Holmes said. True professionals are always committed to doing their best job, independent of the rewards. They would be just as committed to creating the best result even if they made less money. Nor would they perform any better if they were paid more money. Return on investment is simply not the point of professionalism.

If an organization hopes to involve people in its cause, then two factors must be in place:

- The organization must be motivated by creating a vision; the desired state must be clear.

- The organization must encourage its members to shift from a focus on return on investment, to a focus on the desired results of the organization.

Once this shift takes place, members of the organization can sign on wholeheartedly. Their involvement becomes a matter of choice, not compliance. They are able to be clear, objective, focused, and collaborative with each other in ways that seemed impossible before. Opinionated people suddenly can review current reality objectively. Moreover, they become interested in each others' opinions, not as an attempt to manipulate the opposition into agreeing with them, but to understand why others see the situation differently and what can be learned from the difference. The actions they take lead to learning, which leads to increased competence and professionalism.

When our prime motivation is to see our desired result become a reality, we are more able to be completely involved with our endeavors, something that would be impossible if our prime focus were on ROI.

Focus on the Outcome

Members can be motivated by the prospect of a return on investment, or because they care about the result itself. The test is this: What is the *primary* driving force?

There often is great return on investment when we play the game for the sake of the game. We might become rich, influential, or famous, but while these rewards might be welcome, *they would not be the point of the involvement.* They might be an appreciated side effect, but not our reason to act. For most of us a paycheck is necessary to fund our activities. If we are not independently wealthy, we have to keep body and soul together. But salary is not usually the *prime* motivation for the type of work we choose to do. There are other reasons, and the most powerful is because we want to see our vision exist in reality.

This type of motivation may sound idealistic, but it is not. For many people, particularly the very accomplished ones, it is the reason they do what they do. All great things are done for their own sake. Leaders who can tap into that aspect of human nature are able to guide people to reach for that which is highest in them.

Emotional Return on Investment

Self-esteem and satisfaction are two forms of emotional return on investment that are used by organizations to motivate their members.

Self-Esteem

With the advent of pop-psychology, the self-esteem craze has hit the ground running within many organizations. The idea is simple enough: People do what they do to feel good about themselves. This is a form of emotional return on investment, and it assumes that if people can increase their sense of self-esteem, personal performance will improve. This also assumes that people's lives revolve around the need for personal reinforcement of their precarious identities.

According to this theory, we are so emotionally needy that we crave the glorious reinforcement of managerial praise and thus will increase our performance at the drop of a "Well done!"

But shifts in our emotional life occur at regular intervals. Sometimes we feel better than other times. If our involvement is determined by our emotional state, what do we do on bad days? Can a manager be expected to provide authority in the inner lives of those who are managed? Of course not.

If we acted only for the purpose of bolstering our egos, it would be difficult for us to be involved with our work. We would devalue the very thing that is being done. Motivation by self-esteem inadvertently says that the creation itself doesn't really matter so long as it strokes the ego. Yet how can we involve ourselves in something that doesn't matter? We can't.

If we were to translate this message more accurately around the organization, the walls would be filled with slogans that read "What you are doing within this organization is only incidental to what really matters—how you feel about yourself."

Managers often find that their attempts to implement the self-esteem notion work against professionalism and learning, because standards become personal and subjective rather than organizational and objective.

If our goal were merely an emotional return on investment, it would be difficult to address our mistakes and inadequacies, and they may have to be addressed, to get the job done and to provide the individual and organization with essential learning.

Satisfaction

A close cousin to motivating through self-esteem is motivating through satisfaction. Here, it is assumed that people do what they do to get a sense of satisfaction and fulfillment. Personal satisfaction as a motive again implies that the actual results of our actions do not have intrinsic merit.

Of course we all enjoy a sense of satisfaction when we can have it. But are the great organizational achievements really accomplished by clusters of individuals seeking personal satisfaction? If so, how do we perform on days we are not satisfied?

Many organizations have adopted the idea that their job is to provide satisfaction to their members. This puts the organization at a disadvantage. People are sometimes satisfied, but more often they are not. Satisfaction, while pleasant, is not a virtue, nor is dissatisfaction a vice. It is important to remember that many of the most accomplished people in the history of civilization were not always satisfied individuals.

When either self-esteem or personal satisfaction are used as motivations, they limit involvement to those projects that are likely to bring an emotional return on investment. Why?

1. It is hard to predict what projects will bring personal rewards, therefore motivation is tied to speculation.

2. But perceptions change and as a result, the motivation to stay with a particular project drifts into inconsistencies.

3. Emotional rewards devalue the intrinsic worth of the involvement itself.

4. Unclear performance standards lead to subjective evaluations of reality (how it feels rather than how it is), which makes learning, evaluating, adjusting, and improving difficult.

Control

Many managers seem to be motivated by an almost obsessive desire for control. This is definitely out of vogue these days, and so the desire for control is generally sublimated into behavior that is more socially acceptable. In many cases, the obsession has simply gone underground.

Since the focus within many organizations is on behavior, rather than the causes of behavior, a person with a control strategy is criticized without being understood. The person attempts to change—to be more open to others, to be more inclusive, to trust people, to let go of many tightly held controls—but over time the person reverts back to the controlling state because the underlying structures in the person's life or in the life of the organization do not support a behavior change of this type. Before a structural change can be achieved we must understand what gives rise to the behavior.

Why do people want control? Are they, at heart, power-hungry dictators that secretly want to rule the world? Are they psychologically depraved, needing to complete their relationships with their fathers or mothers? Are they overly ambitious and calculatingly insensitive? Probably not.

Why do managers gravitate toward controlling behavior? First, because of certain unexplored assumptions that they hold to be true. These assumptions are one element of the structure. The other reasons are the person's aspirations and values, and the reality itself. Of these three reasons, the assumptions need to be explored in depth. Indeed if the assumptions by a person with a control strategy were true, it would make sense to adopt this strategy.

These assumptions are:

1. There is a potential for danger and therefore negative consequences may occur.

2. People cannot be trusted—perhaps their integrity can be, but certaintly not their judgment.

3. If people were left to their own devices, they might create great harm. Therefore people must be protected from harm they may not even know exists. The manager (or whomever else holds these assumptions) must take charge for the greater good of everyone.

Those who have a control strategy do not think of themselves as others may see them, as manipulative and power-wielding. These people see themselves as good people who are simply misunderstood. They do not want power or control; they just want to protect everyone. And they feel that letting go of their power will lead to harm. Since they are motivated by a fear of negative consequences, telling them to change their ways does little to change their strategies.

For us to understand such people, we must not presume that they are in love with power. Often they do not want to be controlling at all. To gain insight into the causes of their behavior, we need to explore reality together and address their assumptions.

Fear of Negative Consequences.   Every situation has a potential for danger whether we act or not, but what is the reality of the danger? *To a person who has a control strategy, danger is conceptualized.* It is imagined. The imagination simply takes over and produces more and more conflict about what could go wrong. Even real danger is translated into a concept. The concept is used as a substitute for reality. To people with a control strategy, the danger they experience seems real but the experience is imagined.

Any of us who are parents have experienced this. We imagine our children falling off a roof, having a bike accident, burning down the house, drowning in the pool, and on and on. While dangers do exist, our fear of them is not usually steeped in reality, but rather in our *concept* of reality. Controlling parents love their children and only want to protect them from harm. But often they have lost touch with reality.

What *is* reality? How much actual danger *is* there? People who have control strategies are not used to seeing reality objectively. In most cases, their sense of danger comes not from looking at reality but from not looking at it. By staying in touch with reality more of the time, the tendency to control can quickly evaporate. This is as true for the manager as it is for the parent.

Distrust of Others.   Again, the *concept* dominates the perception. What people can't we trust? When? How? Why not? In reality, some people can be relied upon more than others. But the controlling person doesn't know who can be trusted and who can't. When the stakes seem so high based on conceptualized danger, the person is unwilling to take a chance.

Here again reality is the only place to go. What is the truth about specific individuals? After exploring reality, the controlling person can often judge people individually rather than tarring everyone with the same brush.

The issue of trust is best explored after the true *reality* of danger has been addressed. If the controlling person imagines a looming threat everywhere, no other person, no matter how reliable he or she may have been in the past, can be counted on. Therefore it is useful to see reality for what it is rather than encouraging people to have blind faith.

Assumption of Superiority.   "People do not know what is in their best interest," the controlling person thinks. This type of person is often quite protective of the rest of us. Our safety is seen as more important than our freedom, and they are certain their choices are superior to those of others.

When we study reality rigorously, we learn that there are certain things that are beyond our control. Many things in life are simply out of the realm of human choice.

Controlling people do not know this. Instead, particularly as they get older, they attempt to control more and more of their world. But reality, being what it is, often defeats their best efforts. They experience a growing sense of powerlessness, which leads in turn to an increased sense of threat and a greater fear of the future. This gives them even more reason to control anything they can. This futile cycle leads to less ability to act effectively, to create desired outcomes, and to help the organization build increased capacity. Over time, the controlling person's strategy defeats growth, learning, and even his or her own sense of stability.

Organizations have control strategies for the same reasons individuals have them. They fear negative consequences. Change can seem threatening. To control the unpredictable, policies are put forward to anticipate what might happen and how the organization should respond. Control is often expressed in an array of policies, rules, and regulations designed to be used in the face of any new situation.

Another more subtle control strategy involves class distinctions. In some organizations, roles are defined and spelled out in detail so that people will know their place. There are penalties for not obeying the rules. Ethics are clearly defined, because it is presumed that people do not have proper values and would only do the "right thing" if forced into it by an ethical code determined by the organization.

Motivation Through Symbols

More and more these days, organizations attempt to motivate people by using symbols; thus awards and fancy titles have become common.

Symbols are not reality, nor are they the playing field of real accomplishment. *Symbols are simply pictures that have been given synthetic meaning.*

Symbols can lead us away from reality, rendering us impotent and ineffective because we are farther from understanding what reality actually is.

Personal versus Organizational Motivation

Within most organizations, reward systems are constructed to reinforce individual performance. How are we to know if the performance is worth rewarding? How can we reward individuals when some of the best work is done by groups without individual fanfare? Indeed the best groups are so unified in their performance that the individual contributions are integrated into a seamless whole. In the arts this is called *ensemble*.

The following illustration shows the structural conflict between the need for personal credit and the requirements for organizational team performance:

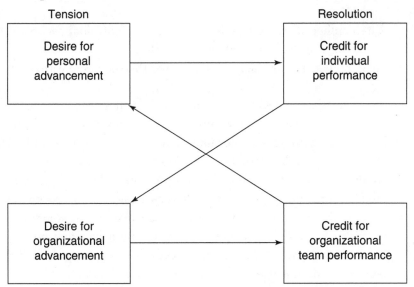

Obviously, there are competing tendencies. The desire for personal advancement leads to a desire to stand out as an individual (how can we shine?). But this conflicts with the need of the team to flourish as a group.

Our cultural traditions and educational system reinforce the idea of individual success, as demonstrated by personal victory, triumph, and even conquest. But often group skills are needed to advance an organization.

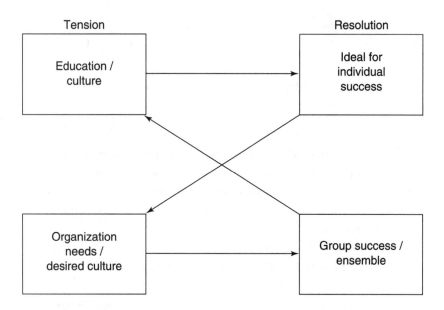

The conflict of interest between group and individual success is usually built into the organizational structure. But with a structural redesign, both elements can reinforce, rather than compete with, each other.

As we have seen, structural conflicts such as these can be resolved by establishing hierarchies of importance and values. When we determine which element is of senior importance and which is secondary, we are able to establish structural tension as the dominant force.

Which is more important—the group or the individual? To help us think about this, we can make a "forced choice" to better define our values. If we had to choose between personal kudos, where our accomplishment would not help the group, or group accomplishment, where we would not get any personal accolades, which would it be? Of course, we do not usually face this kind of extreme choice; however, it is a useful thought experiment. Once we know where we stand, we can establish hierarchies, and they will be based on our most important values.

Mishmash of Motivations

Because people have various concepts about what motivates others, confusing and inconsistent policy designs, reward systems, and managerial reinforcements fill the organization. The illustration at the bottom of this page charts the type of compensation that various people may use if they thought that employees were motivated by particular needs or desires. Notice how wide the differences are. Imagine what might happen when there are mismatches.

Perhaps the human resources department thinks that people are motivated by praise. They tend to hire people who seem interested in acclaim. Once hired, these people might find that they work for a boss who thinks people are motivated by threat, conflict, and pressure. The mismatch creates a wider and wider gap between manager and team member. Or perhaps a person who is motivated by symbols works for a person who thinks people are motivated by financial gain. The boss gives the employee a raise, expecting that money is all that is needed to motivate the person. But, to that person, money alone may be a poor symbol. Conflicts develop because motivational concepts are not matched to reality, nor to the real desires of the organization as expressed in its purpose, strategies, and goals.

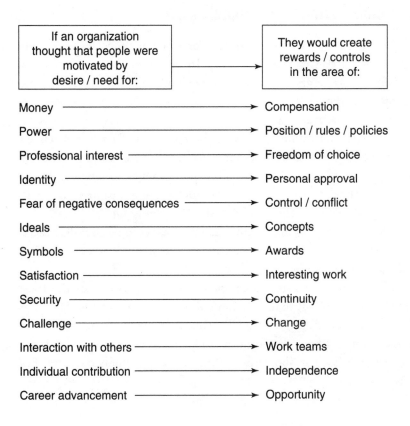

If an organization thought that people were motivated by desire / need for:	They would create rewards / controls in the area of:
Money	Compensation
Power	Position / rules / policies
Professional interest	Freedom of choice
Identity	Personal approval
Fear of negative consequences	Control / conflict
Ideals	Concepts
Symbols	Awards
Satisfaction	Interesting work
Security	Continuity
Challenge	Change
Interaction with others	Work teams
Individual contribution	Independence
Career advancement	Opportunity

In some organizations, people are forced to seek managerial titles because that is the only means for promotion leading to higher pay. Some people who do not want to be managers become managers anyway. In a few organizations, individual contributors who do not manage anyone may be given a managerial *title* so they can qualify for promotion and increased benefits. This type of system seems to value managers rather than individual contributors.

When managing a project team or a department, scientists or engineers may be so hungry to participate in the actual science or technology being developed that they sometimes interface with team members in ways that create dissension and confusion. Many project managers hope the departmental manager will stop interfering with the project, but many individual members hope the project manager will *manage* rather than try to do the hands-on work. Being a manager in this type of organization removes people from the work they actually love, and creates a conflict.

The High-Performance Organization

The organizations that consistently produce high performance are those with a consistent motivation. In addition, the motivations of individuals are aligned with each other and with that of the organization as a whole.

Not all motivations work equally well to produce high performance. The motivation that works best individually and collectively is a focus on the desired outcome rather than on various forms of return on investment. In the highest-performance groups within the worlds of sport, the arts, science, technology, and business, the focus is always directly on the results desired by the group.

Here is the most important question concerning any discussion about motivation: *Can an organization influence the motivation of its individual members?*

The answer for a given company can point to one of the most telling insights about that company's future. We cannot simply say yes or no. If the organization is unclear about its motivation, values, and goals, it will not have the authority to lead and motivate others. If the organization is clear about these things, it can influence others. But it is a big job.

How the organization can influence motivation:

- Be clear about its own motivation.

- Have a continuous educational process that reinforces its motivation.

- Construct rewards that consistently reinforce its motivation.

- Consciously orchestrate its hiring practices.

- Demonstrate its values through its actions.

- Dedicate resources toward creating an organization-wide alignment.

- Walk the talk and talk the truth about where the organization stands.

Until we can distinguish between the *doer* and *that which is done*, the topic will always seem overly complex and mysterious. Once we make that distinction, however, we can understand this simple insight: When people truly care about outcomes, they can reach greater heights of accomplishment than previously thought possible. When this motivation is joined to a well-structured organization, the organization will be capable of extraordinary performance.

Quick Review

- Without understanding what truly motivates people to reach for that which is highest and best in them, rewards can be designed that are disincentives.

- There are two very different types of motivations people have—one in which payback and return on investment is the point of the action, the other in which action is taken for the sake of that which is done. The second form of motivation can lead to real involvement; the first cannot.

- Emotional return on investment weakens involvement. Self-esteem and personal satisfaction are forms of this.

- Managers who use a control strategy are motivated by a fear of negative consequences. The best way to address this is to study reality more accurately, so that the manager can go beyond a concept of reality, into clear observations. Telling such a manager simply to stop being controlling will not work.

- Organizations, like some managers, can have control strategies for the same reason. Clarity of reality helps this situation.

- Organizations often have a mishmash of reward systems that create confusion about what is expected and what its values are.

- If organizations build reward systems that reinforce their values and aspirations, and if they eliminate those rewards that contradict those factors, they can better reinforce what they want.

CHAPTER 16

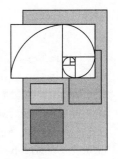

The Learning Organization

With the publication of his book *The Fifth Discipline*, Peter Senge popularized the notion of the learning organization. Since its release, the phrase *learning organization* has become a household word. The notion of a learning organization is a very attractive proposition, indeed. It conjures up images of groups of people working together to increase organizational intelligence, comprehension, and capacity. But what is a learning organization?

Aristotle believed that any universal class that can be characterized by a common noun is a subjective notion and not a tangible reality. To him, universal notions such as *humanity* do not truly exist, except in our thoughts. He considered group classifications to be handy mental abstractions, but hardly external realities. For him, reality is found in individual human beings. Each person is the *actuality*, and the group identity is merely a convenient conceptual construct that doesn't really exist.

To Aristotle, the organization would not really exist except in our imagined abstraction. If he is right, there could not be a learning organization, for what would be doing the learning? *He would answer that only the individual can be a learner.*

Is there a reality to the popular notion of the learning organization, or is the concept a mental invention that does not exist?

Plato thought that universal categories have a greater objective reality than the individual. He argued that the universal is more lasting, important, and substantial than the individual. He wrote, "Men come and go—but mankind goes on forever."

Two interesting viewpoints. We can agree with *both* of them when we consider the organization. Without the individual, there is no organization. The organization cannot be separated from individuals, but individuals can be separate from the organization. Therefore, the individual has a reality independent from the organization, while the organization can only exist by the participation of actual people. The organization by itself would have no objective reality by aristotelian standards.

On the other hand, it seems that organizations have lives of their own. They are almost like organic entities that are governed by their own principles of movement, growth, possibility, and tendency. People come and go, but the organization can exist with a different cast of characters and outlive them all.

So what is the objective reality of the organization? Within the organization, individual elements (departments, customer demand, manufacturing capability, managerial systems, economic realities) connect and lead to a greater system of relationships. This is analogous to a person, whose cells join together to form a body, and whose body joins with nonphysical elements such as personality, emotion, mind, and spirit, to form a human being.

Whether or not there is an organization in the objective aristotelian sense of reality, the combination of the various organizational elements does seem to function as a single entity and act in accord with its own inescapable structural laws. These laws are so compelling that individuals, when in the organization, act in ways that are consistent with its structure.

The organization has a type of personality and a type of orientation toward the world. It has its own set of values that are expressed through its actions. It has underlying structures that lead to tendencies for behavior, both functional and dysfunctional. The organization does change over long periods of time; such change is often similar to the evolutionary cycle of youthful vigor into serene old age.

Yet the organization can renew itself and become young again, regaining its vitality and drive. It can become rejuvenated—but only if it can learn.

Organizations that can't learn, can't change. Organizations that can learn, can transform themselves into new entities capable of greater heights of achievement.

The Old School: Individual Learning

For most of the postwar period, learning within an organization was primarily done by senior management, who grappled with the deeper managerial and business issues, balanced the competing forces, broke new ground of management technique, and so on. Senior management did most of the thinking for the corporation, which was reflected in the old saying "The people on top do the thinking, the rest of the people in the organization do the acting." Senior management functioned as a think tank, and the rest of the organization worked on implementation.

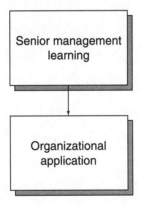

This division of labor worked fairly well when the people on top were *actually* learning. But, as is human nature, many senior executives gradually stopped learning; they began to see themselves as so knowledgeable about their own businesses that no one could teach them anything. During the late sixties and seventies, Detroit automakers were convinced that they knew their business better than anyone else.

Even when senior management in an organization continued to learn, the learning did not always move into the rest of the organization. Individual learning is a good first step, but often individual learning has not led to organizational learning.

A change in one cell of the human body may be an isolated event with no effect on the fundamental structure of the body. Similarly, the enlightenment of one individual or group of individuals may not lead to fundamental organizational enlightenment in general.

The New School: The Learning Organization

A learning organization is not merely a loose federation of individuals who have a high regard for learning and who happen to be part of the same organization. Rather, the learning organization is an entity with the capacity, instinct, and inclination to learn. It is an organization in which learning is everyone's job, an organization alive with the possibility that something new can be born and grow to maturity. The learning is self-generating, neither a product of desperate survival needs that force people into compliance, nor a fad that is quickly taken on and just as quickly abandoned.

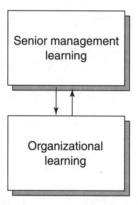

Steven Spielberg's production company is an example of a real learning organization. Many of the principal technical people have been with Spielberg for years. Over that time, people have increased their ability to work and learn together; they learn from each other and learn as a group.

What motivates the learning? In the case of a film company, it is the individual film that is being created.

Learning does not happen in a vacuum, especially within organizations. When learning is tied to a desired end result, it becomes an essential part of the process that produces the result. Learning becomes relevant to increased capacity, intellectual capital, and organizational competence.

Many of the great Japanese companies use learning as part of their business strategy, which gives them a tremendous competitive advantage. They may introduce a new product—a cellular phone, a copier, a lap top computer, a synthesizer—products using new technology that is not well developed when the product is first released. They support the product group, even when it doesn't make a profit. Over the next number of years, they perfect the product group, learning how to make it better, inventing new technology that improves its performance. By continually experimenting, adjusting, and learning, they master their fields.

The product may not make a profit at first, but eventually it does. Many Western companies would not tolerate a product group that did not make a profit. They would get it off the market and perhaps even leave the industry. But the great Japanese companies understand that short-term profit or loss is only a temporary condition and that learning from involvement in technological development will pay off over time. Being in the market teaches them how to develop the market. It provides ongoing feedback to the developers about the actual needs of the customers. Each new generation incorporates improvements that are relevant to the customer's use of the product, making it more valuable and desirable.

Learning comes in the form of continually improving an imperfect product group or technology—fixing it until they get it right. Once they get it right, they continue to drive the technological development even further.

Learning becomes the key factor in growing a product group or a technology. From early and unpretentious beginnings a company can dominate an industry by learning over time. It takes a lot of time to accomplish this learning, and it takes strategic investment in the future, something that would be impossible if forced to address short-term financial goals.

Why People Learn

There are many reasons why people learn, and some reasons are more conducive to organizational learning than others. Some are more apt to be self-generating and some are not. Learning has a personal dimension that must be considered when forming a learning organization.

Learning for Its Own Sake

Jacob Bronowski, author of *The Ascent of Man*, has said that if a child is anything, he or she is a learning machine. By the age of three, children are learning and perfecting their language skills, their motor responses, and their understanding of time and space. They have a natural instinct to learn. Is this a temporary phenomenon, or is it an essential part of the human condition?

People love to learn, and a great deal of learning is not directed toward the accomplishment of anything in particular. Many people, for example, cherish collecting trivial information. They may enjoy knowing Ted Williams' 1948 batting average, or how many dresses Madonna wears during a rock concert. This learning has no practical purpose (except perhaps to annihilate one's opponent in a game of Trivial Pursuit!).

There is something inexplicably enriching about learning facts, theories, computer systems, or details of historical events. This kind of learning is done for pleasure. The point of learning is one's own recreation; it does not *have to* lead to anything more productive or useful, although occasionally it does.

Learning for the sake of learning sometimes results in something new—an invention, a concept, a product, a method—but if this happens it is serendipitous. Learning for the sake of learning could not, by its nature, be the basis of a *reliable* process. Therefore, this is not the type of learning that would lead to a learning organization. Nonetheless, learning of this sort has its own pleasures and individual rewards.

Learning in Order to Solve Problems

Much learning, especially organizational learning, is designed to solve problems. Learning based on problem solving is a defensive type of learning. It is learning how to stop what you don't want. Like the structure of problem solving itself, the incentive to learn is tied to the intensity of the problem: The more intense the problem, the more incentive to learn; the less intense the problem, the less incentive to learn. Once the problematic condition that stimulates learning is ended, the motivation to learn decreases.

There is much confusion about the link between learning and problem solving, especially since problem solving is such a common management technique. But, clearly, *chronic* problem solving within an organization demonstrates a *lack* of essential learning.

In one high-tech company with which we worked, the engineers assigned to customer service loved solving technical problems so much that they saw every situation as a new personal challenge, even if that particular technical problem had already been solved a dozen times before by other engineers. Naturally, the company began to get complaints from their customers. Finally, senior management intervened and made sure all such technical support information was systematized. Learning that had been made on a personal level now became learning for the tech service division as a whole. (Common sense, of course. But it was not at all obvious to the engineers who, ironically, had previously thought they *were* in a learning organization because of all the learning that was going on.)

The personal technical challenge enjoyed by the engineers was in conflict with the goals of the organization. For there to be change, the engineers had to understand the desired end goal of the organization, which was to have highly satisfied customers. Their love of problem solving had to take a back seat to their commitment to the organization's goals, and learning had to become collective and focused.

This still did not make this company a learning organization, in that learning was not self-generated and was generated by managers senior to the engineers. Their orientation was problem based, and their learning was still limited to problem solving. To create a true learning organization, the engineers would have had to become self-generating learners, and then they would have been in a perfect position to discover what the designers needed to know for the next generation of products. In a true learning organization, the learning can migrate in this fashion to those who can apply it best.

Learning for Competitive Advantage

Many organizations are interested in learning these days because the learning organization has a distinct competitive advantage over other types of organizations. But are true learning organizations motivated by a thirst for competitive advantage, or is that simply part of the strategic mix?

Competitive advantages come and go. You may have the competitive advantage in your industry for a few years, only to find that your edge vanishes with the appearance of another company's product line or marketing campaign. Having a superior product should be a competitive advantage, but consider the companies that lost out to other companies that had inferior products but better organizations, organizations able to make those products attractive to more people over a sustained period of time.

Learning in order to gain a competitive advantage supports general learning. But it alone cannot be the basis for a learning organization.

Learning to Ensure Your Own Survival

Some people are of the opinion that if they do not grow, they will not survive. The phrase most often used to express this idea is "Grow or die." Learning connected with this notion results in a defensive position. Of course, when threatened by a strong competitor or our own incompetence, the survival of the organization may indeed come into question. But the learning that results from this motivation will be short lived, and once the crisis is over, the reason to learn is less compelling. As Robert Frost so aptly put it, "I never tried to worry anyone into intelligence." Concern about one's own survival forms a problem-driven structure, and therefore the behavior that results will oscillate over time. This could hardly be the basis of organizational learning.

Learning in Order to Expand Capacity

Learning is a way to add capacity to an organization at hardly any cost. Training, consulting, computer / laser assisted learning, books, and films are some of the formal means by which an organization can add to its intellectual capacity, increasing the general competence of the organization. And there are informal ways as well, such as on the job learning focused toward improving performance, systems, and strategies.

Training

Training is a powerful instrument for change, and for strengthening and extending capacity. However, most companies do not appreciate the opportunity that their training departments could provide. Partly this is due to the lack of a clear direction within the training department. Training programs, like reward systems, tend to be put together haphazardly, piecemeal.

Too often, training does not have a clear purpose that is integrated into a comprehensive organizational business and management design. People get training that may be irrelevant. Sometimes training contradicts earlier training that people have been given within the same curriculum.

Most often, training is seen as separate from the business strategy and the management strategy. The organization knows it is somehow good to have training, but it doesn't truly understand how powerful a resource it can be because training, and learning in general, is conceived of as being outside the context of the real work of the company.

For a training method to be successful, it must reinforce both the management and business strategies by developing relevant skills, by driving new ways the organization can learn to think, by creating efficient methods to distribute learning throughout the organization, and by unifying the organization's cultural and intellectual foundation.

In work with many training departments, our company has helped redesign their training approach so that it could reinforce the overall goals and strategies of the organization. Here are some of the rudiments to developing a relevant training program:

1. Define the general business strategy.

2. Define how the managerial strategy supports it.

3. Define the training goals in relationship to the business and management strategy.

4. Divide training into basic and specialized functions.

5. Evaluate the current offering.

6. Eliminate training that is inconsistent with the overall strategy.

7. Add training that reinforces the overall strategy.

8. Design an overall curriculum.

9. Market the new comprehensive training strategy in-house.

10. Stay in close touch with various managerial levels to moni tor the success of the approach and adjust the approach as needed.

Making Training Relevant

Many people think of training as classroom learning. But it can and should be much more than that. For training to be directly useful, it must translate into real work-related actions. If a manager takes a course and walks away with useful concepts that cannot be directly applied, from the organizational point of view the training method has failed.

The best possible training is on-the-job. When limited to course work, training can seem abstract and theoretical. Yet many training departments offer an assortment of courses that are barely translat able into work-related applications. At the end of the exercise, peo ple feel that training, while perhaps interesting, is not a terribly good investment of their time.

In one of our client's companies, the training department revamped its entire approach and developed a comprehensive cur riculum leading to three types of in-house MBA programs. Their train ing method went from a confused mix of contradictory course offer ings, to a streamlined and effective learning strategy that reinforces the business and organizational strategies.

As consultants, we study the company's business strategy and values, develop a list of characteristics that are important to the organization, and evaluate every existing training program: Does it support the overall business and management strategies? We then develop training goals in each area and tie them directly into the general business strategy.

Once this design work is done, we meet with many of the key players who would be the end users in this integrated approach, and we received valuable feedback and insights. They often offer to help pilot the new approach toward training.

Training becomes useful to the organization in new ways. In one case, the process represented a major shift in the company's approach, from a catalogue-based style of unrelated courses, to a comprehensive training strategy related to vital business and organizational issues. This redesign was also cost effective. The training department was able to produce a much better training program for about $200,000 *less* than its original budget.

To most people, expanding capacity is a matter of adding more people or buildings, computer systems or machinery. But one commonly missed way of adding capacity is helping people improve their ability to work together. Many managers think managerial skills are simply a matter of common sense or intuition. Perhaps, having attended many less-than-useful management training courses, they cannot conceive of training as helpful to them. However, the right type of training can be as critical in adding capacity to the organization as adding new factories or technology.

When used as part of the entire organizational strategy, training is a powerful resource that can help an organization reach heights of achievement previously unimagined, and do so in the most cost effective way possible.

Learning in order to expand capacity is useful, and, while that factor alone will not lead to the creation of a learning organization, it is an essential ingredient of the whole picture. As organizations begin to explore the terrain of the learning organization, new systems may be adopted that lead to change, and a good test of the efficacy of these new systems is their effect on capacity.

Creation of Desired Results

Probably the best reason to learn is to produce the results we want. The best reason for an organization to become a learning organization is its desire to achieve tangible goals. The goals may be specific business goals, like bringing a product to market, or they may be more general goals, like giving customers access to a new product line or service.

More than any single motivation, the desire to create something meaningful encourages learning at its best. This learning is highly functional and fashioned to our aspirations. It helps us learn material, even when it is inconvenient, difficult, and complicated. It helps us face the reality of our current abilities or conditions (which may be less desirable than we would like to admit), and from the true starting point of our current competence we can grow, mature, and develop.

Creating results that matter to us gives learning a focused purpose. The learning is self-generating because people want to master the skills, principles, and proficiencies that will help them accomplish their aims. They also want to learn about the current circumstances in ways they may have avoided in the past. Detrimental habits are changed or overcome. People consistently rise to the occasion, and then begin to learn that they can count on each other.

We can describe the characteristics of a learning organization once it exists, but we cannot produce a learning organization by taking on those characteristics, any more than if we looked wistfully into someone's eyes and sighed repeatedly we could fall in love. The learning organization is really a by-product of a well-structured organization, not a direct product of it.

Experiment in Creating a Learning Organization

During one Brenton Woods Conference on the learning organization, I co-led a workshop called "The Essence Behind Learning." At one point, we asked people to form into groups of five. We then gave them seven minutes to become "a learning organization." That was their only direction. They were on their own as to how they would do it. After time was up, we asked the groups to report on what had happened.

Most groups reported similar experiences: the individuals had gotten to know each other and had formed a strong sense of personal relationships, but seven minutes was too short a time to create a learning organization. At first, many people did report learning something, but when they were asked "What did you learn?" it turned out that they had only confirmed impressions already held.

Later in the workshop, we gave same-size groups an exercise requiring them to create something together. One member of the group was designated as the "sculptor," and the other members were "performers," the raw materials for the piece the sculptor would create. Their job was to help the sculptor produce the result he or she wanted.

Before the sculptors went to work, we asked them to close their eyes and conceive of the piece they were about to create. We asked them to form a general picture of it. Will it tell a story? Will it be abstract? Where are the contrasts? Where is it more active, and where is it less active? Within thirty seconds, each sculptor formed a concept of his or her piece. Once that step in the exercise was completed, we gave them two minutes to put the piece together.

After two minutes, time was called and the performers held their positions. The sculptors moved away from their pieces, visited the other pieces, and then, finally, came back to their own piece.

Then each group broke position, and another member became the sculptor. Eventually, each person had a chance to be the sculptor. The pieces were magnificent and everyone was amazed at their creations.

During the discussion following this exercise, people reported having had a tangible experience of being a learning organization or a learning group. The learning was self-generated and collective as well as individual. The learning increased over each of the two-minute projects and over the entire course of the exercise.

The contrast between the earlier "create a learning organization" exercise and the "create a sculpture" exercise was dramatic. One produced a lot of talk about the learning organization, but did not produce one. The other produced a learning organization without any talk about learning.

The Role of Structural Tension

During the "create a sculpture" exercise, the sculptors used all the steps of a creative process most commonly used by professional creators (filmmakers, composers, painters, novelists). In other words, they created *structural tension*. They began with a *general concept* of a desired end result. As they added more detail to their initial concept, it evolved into a more tangible *vision*. Then they went back to their groups and observed the *current reality* (people standing around). The discrepancy between the desired state (their vision) and the actual state (the current reality) then formed a *tension*. They then took *action* as they positioned the performers as needed. How did they make decisions during this process? The actions produced change, which they *evaluated*, using the discrepancy between the vision and reality as the standard of measurement. They then made *adjustments* as needed. This was a continual learning process—learning what worked and what didn't. They brought the piece to *completion* by putting finishing touches on their pieces, and then asking the performers to hold their positions. This *resolved* the tension they had formed in the beginning of the process because the discrepancy between the desired state and the actual state no longer existed. They then became the *audience* for their own piece.

This process, used almost universally in the arts, is also supremely well suited to organizations. To many, words like *creative process, creativity* and *creating* produce images of impractical starving artists in lofts. Or, as thought of in organizational life, simple idea generation. These images are misleading, for the actual creative process is the most effective process ever devised for accomplishment. Therefore, it must be practical and workable.

The power of the creative process is found in the structure it establishes—structural tension. Structural tension is a structure that is able to resolve. It does not lead to oscillation. By its nature, it is a structure that leads to self-correcting adjustments and learning as a natural part of the process. Within the frame of structural tension, a consistent pattern of learning takes place (see illustration, next page).

Organizations that understand that their business is *creating results*, and that therefore the creative process is their major means to accomplish those results, are well positioned to succeed by designing their organization to structurally advance.

Organizational Focus

Another insight by the people involved in the sculpture exercise was their relationship to time and focus. Most people were finished before the two minutes were over. Their focus was on the sculpture they were

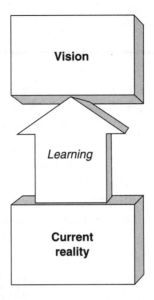

creating and not on their moods, their identities, their emotions, or even on how well they might do. As they worked on the sculpture, they experienced growing momentum, so that learning accelerated and actions became more effective and easier. They were fully involved.

They reported two experiences of time during the exercise: an atmosphere of timelessness and an incredible, laser-like focus on each moment. They experienced great affinity for the other members of the group and felt that they could be counted on.

The performers also experienced a high level of involvement, growing momentum, accelerated learning, and heightened focus. During our discussion afterwards, people reported that it didn't matter to them whether they were the sculptor or the performer because they were all working toward the same result. They all wanted the project to be a success. They also experienced a sense of community with the other members of the group.

These are not the sentiments commonly found among the members of most organizations. Why was this short exercise able to create this type of alignment so quickly and naturally? Because working within the frame of structural tension gives rise to a predictable and consistent pattern of collaborative behavior.

It would be impossible to build a learning organization without also building a *creating* organization based on structural tension.

A Learning Orientation

Learning is not limited to an activity that one does now and then. It can be a way of life, an *orientation*.

In my book *Creating* I first made a distinction between a learning orientation and a performing orientation. Most of us—to the detriment of our learning process—have been raised to be performers. Our schools reinforce the performing orientation by rewarding us for performance *over* learning. If you do well on a test but have learned nothing, you get an A. If you do not do well on a test, but learn a great deal, you may get a C, D, or even an F. Traditional education compensates us for high performance, not high learning. Evaluation is not based on learning.

We can tell if an organization has a performance orientation rather than a learning orientation by the way it deals with mistakes. In a performance-oriented company, people avoid making mistakes by minimizing risks and minimizing aspirations. Mistakes that do happen are often hidden. People who play it safe succeed, and those who attempt to sail new waters are not encouraged.

An organization with a learning orientation treats mistakes quite differently. While mistake making is not encouraged, the organization realizes that, in reality, people make mistakes. The mistakes they make can be used to learn. This learning leads to higher performance. No organization should risk any of its critical factors. But organizations with a learning orientation understand the nature of experimentation, and they set up places where something new can be tried, but at low risk to the organization if the experiment fails. New projects, approaches, products, technologies, information systems, or management tactics almost always begin their life with flaws. Correction and adjustment are an essential part of the learning process, enabling an organization to far out-perform another organization that has a performance orientation. An organization can improve its own performance over time through the experience of continual learning that is managed and directed toward the formal goals of the company.

The Fate of the Learning Organization

Learning comes in many forms. We learn from our own experiences, or vicariously from the experiences of others. We learn intellectually, culturally, subconsciously, and intuitively. We learn objectively or subjectively. We learn through discovery, observation, experimentation, invention and innovation. Learning can be skill based or conceptual. With so many ways to learn, it is surprising that our educational systems tend to emphasize only one—informational learning.

Many people have the idea that learning means acquiring more and more information. When they consider the concept of a learning organization, they envision an institution in which people are busily amassing more facts, theories, models, systems, and knowledge. It can seem overwhelming. "It's all we can do just to do our jobs," complain people who think that learning is accumulating more and more information. "Who's got time to learn? And if someone does have time, how come? Perhaps they're being negligent." This idea about learning comes from a comparative thought process where people think that learning is adding knowledge to the "database" they use to compare reality.

Do organizations learn in the same way individuals learn? Yes and no. The collective learning process begins with individuals, but then it becomes *more vicarious and less directly experiential.* In fact, this is one of the strengths of the learning organization: The individual learning experiences of a few people are multiplied into a more general, collective learning.

The phrase *learning organization* is in a precarious position just now because of its popularity. To many organizations, it is beginning to sound like yet another fad that will lead to nothing much in the end. This is truly unfortunate, because learning as a way of life for an individual and an organization offers some of the best hope for building the future we want.

Learning in an organization structured to oscillate will widen the magnitude of the oscillation because, as the second law of organizational structure tells us, success in an oscillating organization does not succeed. So learning and the structure of an organization are inextricably tied together. Learning in an organization structured to advance becomes one of the ongoing strengths upon which we can always rely.

Quick Review

- Organizations can renew themselves when they can learn. When they can't learn, they can't change.

- Organizational learning is best motivated when it serves an outcome the organization wants to create.

- Learning in order to expand capacity and learning in order to serve specific organizational aspirations are two good reasons why organizations learn.

- Training is a powerful instrument for change and expanding capacity at very little cost. However, the way training is approached in most organizations fails to take advantage of this opportunity; training is not often tied to the organization's business strategy. When it is, training becomes directly relevant to the organization.

- One of the best ways to create a learning organization is to focus on creating outcomes that matter to the organization. The learning organization is often a by-product of structural tension, rather than a result that is created for itself.

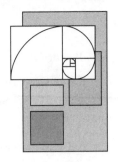

CHAPTER 17

Organizational Greatness

Characteristics of a Great Organization

Once the foundation of an organization has been structured to advance, what can we build upon it? Organizational greatness.

Greatness is not a utopian ideal demanding conformity to a set of prescribed values, goals, or codes for behavior. Rather, it is an organization that continually takes a stand for its values and dreams; an organization in which the highest in the human spirit can be expressed; an organization that continually reaches out to its future. It is certainly not perfect, but in its imperfection lies the seeds of its learning. It is alive, dynamic, and growing, and when we are in its presence, we immediately recognize its heights and depths, for it seems to evoke in us a call to be our best and most noble.

Great organizations are, in microcosm, what great civilizations are in macrocosm. They have a strength of being that goes beyond any individual, but this strength is dependent on the involvement of many individuals. Leadership itself must be great, wise, and dynamic, but the great organization can outlive its leaders, while the lesser organization cannot. Why? What are the elements of organizational greatness?

257

- Power is distributed widely and well.
- Consistent relationships between local interests and overall interests are soundly managed.
- The organization, itself, is a social force.
- Principles determine policies.
- Expansion is clearly defined.
- Resources are managed in ways consistent with the comprehensive design.
- The organization continually aligns people.

Widely Distributed Power

While leadership is essential, it must be able to expand and distribute its power beyond the term of office of any one individual. Alexander the Great was history's first world leader. During his life, he unified the ancient world, first through conquest, then through forming fair and equitable local governments. But, because he was not able to distribute power widely and well, his world fell apart when he died.

Like Alexander, there are great organizational leaders who do not distribute power widely and well. Therefore, while they are able to bring their organizations to a level of greatness while they reign, the organization fades as soon as they are gone.

Greatness begins with human aspiration and values, but that alone cannot be the only basis for organizational greatness. Structural design can take that original impetus for greatness, and build it into interconnected sets of reinforcing relationships in which the distribution of power places strength where it is needed—strategically, tactically, and managerially.

Soundly Managed Relationships

While we live with change as a constant, our ability to manage change is made possible by establishing consistent relationships between the local and overall interests of the organization. Local interests must be brought into alignment with the organization's overall interests. But this alignment cannot be achieved by lapsing into an ad hoc arrangement that demands constant adjustment and correction. It must become an essential part of the structure, so continuity can be established and then built upon, and flexibility can focus change toward meaningful aims.

The Organization as a Social Force

Great organizations do more than perform well financially. They are a social force. CNN, for example, is seen worldwide and has brought the whole world together during times of triumph or peril. Microsoft has become a social force, influencing the ways people use computers. Today we know more and more about the effects of diet on health, and the availability of health foods has had a great impact on society. Cyberspace is more than a social force, it creates its own society. Great organizations within industries such as airlines, telecommunications, or high technology are social (even civilizing) forces. Their opportunities to build a world that can advance is unending.

Great organizations are active members of their civilization. Often this is a by-product of the work they do. However, there is also a high degree of social awareness and the ambition to contribute and help build something better. Sometimes this principle manifests itself in the participation of the organization with the communities where it resides; it can help the economy, enhance quality of life, better the schools, and develop better health care systems, while contributing to cultural enrichment through support of the arts. Other times, the ideas and inventions of great organizations dramatically change people's lives for the better.

Principled Policies

In great organizations, policies are determined by thematic unifying principles and values. It is impossible for an organization to sustain its greatness for long if it has inconsistent or unfair policies, or if policies are improvised by the whim of egocentric managers. Like the rule of law, rather than the prerogative of dictators, when principles determine policies, continuity and fairness can contribute to organizational greatness.

Clearly Defined Expansion

Indiscriminate growth and expansion reveals lack of direction, purpose, and strategy. Great organizations understand that growth is neither a good nor a bad thing in and of itself, and so growth and expansion are always well motivated strategically. Expansion always reinforces the purpose of the organization. It is never arbitrary, mindless, or disconnected from the true aims and governing ideas of the company.

Resource Management Consistent with Overall Design

In this age of cost cutting and downsizing, a mindless feeding frenzy of reducing expenditures has led to chronic organizational folly. In great organizations, resources are managed carefully, because that care creates organizational discipline and an economy of means. All great civilizations managed their resources well, which allowed them to build cities, roads, buildings, and institutions, as well as to defend themselves against their enemies. They invested in their growth wisely, with design and purpose.

These great civilizations declined when they no longer had a vision in which to invest. They began squandering their resources, going through periods of waste followed by periods of cost cutting that eventually dissolved the fabric of their civilization. A parallel cycle is occurring every day in many of our best organizations. While study after study has proven the absurdity of these practices, senior managers seem to be numb to the consequences they are causing.

The organization's resources are seen in its intellectual capital, facilities, people, ideas, spirit, financial capital, and in many other factors that cannot simply be listed but contribute to the resources base of the company. A great organization understands the relationship of these factors to its aims, and never mindlessly dismantles its resources base. Instead, the resources are used to accommodate the organization's ambitions.

Continuing Alignment of People

In Asia, many organizations begin the day with rituals designed to establish and reinforce the governing ideas of the company. In the West, we have morning meetings, newsletters, and video presentations, but we tend to think about alignment informally. The results are often hit and miss. People can fall into and out of alignment. We often assume that once we achieve a degree of accord with people within our organizations, it will continue intact. But it doesn't always.

Shifts in demands can alter a person's focus. When alignment is assumed but unaddressed, we can lose touch with it.

Great organizations create systems that continually align people with their true caring about the governing ideas of the organization. Alignment is never assumed, it is managed.

What is necessary to create alignment?

- People who share the same values

- People wanting to work together toward common outcomes

- People who are members of the organization by their own conscious choice

- People who are motivated by a deep desire to contribute to the organization

- A fair game (one in which people can succeed or fail based on the merits of their actions rather than political intrigue)

When these factors are present, alignment is more possible, but even then, is not guaranteed. The great organizations rekindle alignment by establishing formal methods dedicated to that purpose. It may not be morning rituals in the Asian style, but it serves the same function.

After they mature, organizations often become stodgy and complacent, attempting merely to maintain what they have. Organizations fail when they lose interest in their own aspiration and purpose. Then people have no reason to align.

The great companies stay in touch with the most generative characteristics of the human spirit—invention, exploration, creation, and purpose. Alignment comes from the reality of these qualities.

Structure: Foundation for Greatness

Many of those who built the great organizations understood the inescapable laws of organizational structure instinctively and intuitively, but they were not able to institutionalize them, bring their understanding to a new generation of managers, or enable the organization to think structurally and causally. The weakness of unconscious competence is that it cannot be developed or passed on to new generations.

Quick Review

- Organizational greatness is not a utopian ideal; rather it is found in how an organization takes a stand for its aspirations and values.

- Many great organizational leaders understood the inescapable laws of organizational structure intuitively and instinctually. Unconscious competence limits the ability to expand this understanding throughout the organization.

- To achieve organizational greatness, the following factors must be in place:

  – Power is distributed widely and well.

  – Local interests are managed with overall interests in mind.

  – The organization becomes a social force.

  – Principles determine policies.

  – Expansion is clearly defined.

  – Resources are managed within a comprehensive design.

  – Systems that continually align people are in play.

- Structure is always there for us to see. When people begin to understand and use structure to help them design their organizations, true greatness becomes possible.

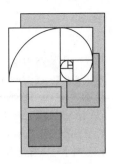

Epilogue

The purpose of this book is to make the inescapable laws of organizational structure, as well as other structural principles and axioms visible so they can be considered, explored, and used in organizational design. When organizations understand these laws and principles, and thereby restructure themselves, they can reach a level of competence, professionalism, achievement, and greatness that has not been within their reach in the past.

Structure is always there for us to see. It is not a model we need to impose on reality, nor is it a belief system we need to develop. It is not a matter of blind faith or metaphor. It is a matter of learning how to see what is *truly* there—the forces in play, the interconnectedness of parts to wholes, the network of relationships that form patterns of behavior.

Once able to see structural relationships, we can begin to understand that many of our previous interpretations and conclusions were not always accurate representations of reality. This type of insight can lead us to wisdom.

It is uncommon for people within organizations to think structurally. This is a situation this book seeks to change, for without a structural understanding, people will make the same mistakes they have always made. They will do their best, but if the structure does not support them, their best efforts will not succeed. When people begin to understand the vast power and beauty of structure, they will no longer be trapped by innocent ignorance. Rather, they will be able to work with the natural forces in play and fulfill their longing to reach for what is highest in them.

Structure is all around us in the natural world. It is dominant in the arts, as well—in every film we see or song we hear. It is in every television commercial we view, and in every rock video on MTV. It is the basis for so much of our world that it is astonishing that it has been so invisible for so long within our organizations. To see it, know it, begin to understand its impact, become able to predict the behavioral patterns it generates, and finally master it so that it can be the basis by which we design our organizations, opens a whole world to us that is rich with possibilities and hope.

The study of structure does not lead us to conclude that the world is merely an indifferent machine, and that our response must be rigid and artificial, unimaginative and sterile. Quite the contrary. The more we study structure, the more we are able to appreciate its splendor and strength, the more we are able to work with it rather than against it, the more we are able to understand that, even within our organizations, Mother Nature is at work.

Understanding structure frees us, not only to imagine new possibilities, but to bring what we envision into reality. It helps us build upon our past, learn from experiences, and also learn from the *future*—once we master the principles of structural cause and effect and can study the probable outcomes the structure harvests.

My hope is this: that individuals and organizations are enriched by knowledge about structure, not only in the tremendously practical realm of performance, but also aesthetically. As the twentieth-century composer Karlheinz Stockhausen has written, "We need to close our eyes for a while and listen. There is always something unheard of in the air."

Knowledge of structural dynamics enables our imagination and aspirations, our values and our hopes, and the depth of our dynamic urge to be the guiding light to the future—to bring about something that heretofore has been "unheard of."

Index

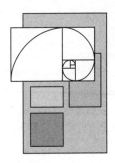

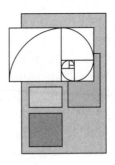

About the Author

For over the past twenty years, Robert Fritz has been developing the field of structural dynamics through his work, first in the area of the creative process, and then in the area of organizational, business, and management issues. He is the founder of *Technologies for Creating* ®, *Inc.* and *The Fritz Consulting Group.*

Fritz began to lead courses in the creative process as applied to personal effectiveness in the mid-seventies. He began to train others to lead his courses, and over 70,000 people have participated in these trainings throughout the world.

His first major discovery was the *macrostructural pattern*, which describes the long-range patterns in people's lives. While each individual's pattern was unique, he observed that there were two general types of patterns that people had in their lives: *oscillating,* and *resolving* or advancing. In the late seventies, he began his work on two basic questions: Why do these patterns exist and what does it take to change them from oscillating to resolving?

These questions led Fritz to pursue deeper questions about the structural make-up of human motivation. His first major book on the subject was *The Path of Least Resistance*, which quickly became a best seller. That was followed by his seond book, *Creating*. These books, along with the TFC trainings, have introduced revolutionary ideas about the influence of structural causality on human beings, both as individuals and within organizations.

In the early eighties, Fritz began to teach consultants the principles of structure in a course called "The Fundamentals of Structural Consulting (FSC)." During the first few years of its existence, over 2,000 people went through the FSC. But the training did not really enable those people to become structural consultants. When Rosalind Hanneman became the London director of TFC–UK, she set out to learn how to master the structural consulting process. She began to notate demonstrations of structural consultations that Fritz would do during training sessions, and then study them until she could understand why each question was asked, and what insight it produced. She continued to practice the fundamental techniques she had learned by using them with her clients, and eventually she began to master structural consulting. Sometime during this period, Fritz and Rosalind Hanneman fell in love, she moved to America, and they married. Rosalind—now Rosalind Fritz—developed the first comprehensive training program in structural consulting, and the first certification in structural consulting was awarded to those who were able to demonstrate professional and technical competence.

As a consultant, Fritz helped many organizations put the structural approach into practice, and his clients include several Fortune 500 companies and many mid-size companies, as well as governmental and nonprofit organizations. Working with other structural consultants, The Fritz Group, Inc. is in the forefront of a revolutionary change in how organizations structure themselves to produce sustained high performance.

Fritz began the study of structure as a composition student at the Boston Conservatory of Music in the sixties. Later he studied compostion in Germany, and was on the faculty of New England Conservatory of Music, and Berklee College. After receiving his BM and MM in composition, Fritz worked as a studio musician in New York and Hollywood, and won positions in *Playboy* and *Downbeat* magazine readers' polls. Fritz is still an active composer, and has written film scores, operas, symphonic music, and chamber music. Most recently, Fritz also has been writing and directing films.

Robert and Rosalind Fritz live in Vermont with their ten-year-old daughter, Eve.

We hope you have enjoyed this book and have found the concepts and principles of value.

If you would like more information about training in structural consulting, the structural consulting services, or software products offered by The Fritz Group, Inc., you may reach us at:

The Fritz Group, Inc.
P.O. Box 249
One River Road
Tipton, PA 16684-0249
Telephone (800) 848-9700
           (802) 348-7176
Fax   (888) 684-2651
           (814) 684-0755
E-mail   info@fritzgroup.com
Web Site: www.fritzgroup.com